Agile Project Management

The Complete Beginner's Guide to Learn Project Management Step by Step

By Eric Lean

Table of Contents

History of Agile Project Management

Before delving into the history of Agile Project Management, it should be noted that *Agile* is not a method. The word *Agile* has been termed as philosophy towards not only software development but product development as well. The philosophy combines well with methods such as Scrum or DSDM, helping to offer an environment that is effective for development.

There's no denying that some highly, positive results have already been delivered by projects that are based on the Agile philosophy when compared to traditional approaches.

History

- **Pre-Agile Period**

During the early 1990s, the enterprise sector began to be proliferated with the help of PC computing, which led to a massive crisis in the development of software. During that time, lag in delivering the applications was critical. It was estimated by the industry leaders that there was a gestation period of at least three years between a business need that was validated and the production of the actual application.

The main problem with this huge gestation period was that in three years since businesses moved and evolved faster, the systems and the requirements of the business were likely to get changed. This led to many projects being canceled halfway through, while some were canceled because they didn't meet the current needs of the business, even if all the original ideas of the project were complied with.

In some industries, the gestation period was far greater than three years. For example, in defense and aerospace engineering, the gestation period was closer to almost twenty years. This was the time taken by a complex system to be moved from the production phase to the action phase. For example, a space shuttle program in the year 1982 used technological information from the 1960s. As the software system goes more complex, the development, design and deployment phase spanned for a couple of years.

This leads us to Jon Kern, who was an aerospace engineer. During the same timeline, he was also growing frustrated with the huge lead times and therefore, the decisions that were taken in his organization earlier could not be modified later. He was looking for a change that leads to more responsive and timely development. Jon Kern along with the seventeen software professionals conducted a meeting. The discussions in the meeting included talking about procedures through which the software development process could be made simpler so that the gestation time could be reduced.

Since other industries during that time were also going through a steep transformation, this was almost a no-brainer. For example, in the automotive industry, companies took at least six years before they implemented a new design. But, during the 1990s, the time was halved to almost three years. The telephone and mobile phone industry were also going through a drastic change since the monopoly of AT&T in the USA was broken.

During that time, the software inside hardware components was basically an afterthought because the development of the software didn't take place until and unless the hardware was designed. This included aircraft, autos, phone switches, and the like. Software development was not a priority for most of the time.

- ## The Birth of Agile Alliance and It's Reasons

Due to all these frustrations growing and mounting one upon the other, the Agile philosophy was born. This was in response to the software development activities which were unproductive, and the same feelings were shared by like-minded professionals as well. This led to the creation of the Snowbird meeting, in Utah, USA, during the year 2001. This was not the first time that these software professionals met together for the development of Agile. In the year 2000, the same group of people also gathered around the Rogue River Lodge, in Oregon, USA, for a massive discussion on the same issue.

The group obviously included Jon Kern, but with him also involved other software professionals such as Ward Cunningham and Kent Beck from Extreme Programming pioneers. Along with them included Alistair Cockburn, Arie van Bennekum and twelve other people. This was known as the *Agile Community* or the *Agile Alliance*. During that time, the word *Agile* was still not used formally. Instead, words like *lightweight* or even *light* were used, which had fitted better with the idea's description.

The creators of this alliance wanted to stress highly on ways to build working software in a quick and precise manner, so that they could be used by the users as fast they can. There were many significant benefits that came with this fast delivery idea or approach. First of all, it helped users to get various benefits from the business with the help of the software faster than ever. The second benefit was that the software developers can get quick feedback from the users, so that bug fixes could be made more rapidly. This will help in shaping the direction and scope of software development.

Some of the important features of the agile movement were that it relied on the willingness and also rapid feedback as well. In any case, the software development team doesn't know what the user needs or wants are, they can build an early BETA version of the software and then listen to user feedback, to further shape the overall project. Agile was all about getting the software shipped out in record time.

- **The Birth Of Agile Project Management**

Over time, Agile Software Development became more and more popular. Therefore, the people or professionals who were involved with activities regarding software development but were not responsible for the creation of such software began to start thinking about implementing the same ideas of Agile in their own line of work.

The Agile Alliance was responsible for the creation of the Agile Manifesto and its 12 principles, which very much started to address the issues that software developers particularly faced. As a mindset, since Agile is a philosophy, the same mindset can also be applied to other fields of activities too. On doing that, Agile will be turned into an adjective. The word Agile describes a way to perform any activity and not any kind of methodology for any of the above-explained reasons.

The following are a few reasons why Agile Project Management was created:

- Use of interactions and individuals over the use of tools and processes.

- Use of a working software rather than a document that seems comprehensive.

- Use of the feedback from the customer rather than the negotiation of a contract.

- Use of a responsive or dynamic plan to react to change rather than following a strict plan.

The Agile Practice Guide was created by the Project Management Institute or PMI along with the Agile Alliance. This guide was created in response to a question that included the need to implement the management of any project in such a way that it can respond, create, change and therefore deal with uncertainty in a much better manner. This will help the project managers to create a product that needs less rework and also requires less risk, but still, meet the needs of the users more often than not.

Some of the core principles of Agile Project Management:

- *Development that is incremental and iterative* - This is a significant factor that stresses on the importance of giving the users along with business managers a simple early glance of all the elements that are to be delivered. This will help in getting the feedback and reviews earlier than expected. This will aid in knowing the interpretation of both the users and the business managers before the project is carried forward by the development team.

- *An effective team is established* - Every Agile project will have a core team that will be effective in planning and carrying out the project. This will help in encouraging interactions between the users, business managers, and developers as well. This is to ensure that everyone's mind is on the same track and the main ambition of the project shouldn't stray far off its final destination.

- *The communication should be effective* - In Agile Project Management, communication should always be face to face. This mode is highly preferred over other modes of communication because it's intimate and always effective. Even though in certain circumstances, face to face communication can be indeed challenging, the main principle can easily be achieved and extended in a number of ways.

It should be kept in mind that *Agile* processes are the essential first steps towards the management of a particular project. Still, the project managers require to implement radical changes to maintain the continuous delivery of the product updates. The managers need to change or remove any features from the product, depending upon the user reactions. These user reactions will not come in the form of words but in the form of actions. Data should be collected on user behavior and real-time analysis should be done on that same data so that the project managers and their teams could know about their next step.

Introduction to Agile Project Management

The word *Agile* can be defined as a methodology for the management of a project which uses developmental cycles that are short and are therefore named as *sprints*, so that focus could be exerted on continuous improvement in the overall development of a service or product.

Agile is an umbrella term used for software development projects like Scrum. Agile Project Management is a specialized method in project management, which is a lot different from conventional methods.

Incremental development methods for software were introduced in the year 1957, while agile was discussed in-depth first in the 1970s. During that time, William Royce had published a research paper on large systems and their software development. Then in the year 2001, the Agile Manifesto was created containing the twelve principles and four values of Agile were introduced. The Agile Manifesto was published by seventeen software engineers.

Agile Project Management can be termed as one of the most revolutionary methods used for the practice of various types of project management. It is one of the latest strategies to be applied to software development projects. The best way to relate Agile Project Management is to combine its technicalities with the development of software. With the overall advancement in the technologies used in software development, developers had to use modern tactics instead of traditional ones. Due to these requirements, the community for information technology created the model for the agile software development project.

The Need to Be Agile

Currently, the 21st century is the age of information. Nowadays, businesses employ workers with knowledge. Workers with knowledge include your peers, colleagues, partners, and the likes, who work together to create great solutions for various social, economic, customer, world and business problems. These workers apply their knowledge, analysis, understanding, reasoning, skills, and expertise to meet the changing demands. Therefore, these workers need techniques and strategies that will not be fulfilled by conventional processes that started in the 1950s. They need something new and extraordinary. This is where the need for Agile arises.

There's no project in the world that can confidently set out from start to finish without any changes being needed. With the help of changes, both risks and opportunities will lead to the success of the project. The difference between a great and a fantastic company can only be defined as the way by which opportunities are taken by the respective companies. In the same way, if risks are not managed in the right way, it can lead to the company's disaster. With the help of agile, change can be managed.

By adopting agile methods and policies, it will allow you to be more responsive to a change in the overall requirements. It will help the development team to be expert at making decisions, which is then supported by trusting, engaged and informed business. It will help you to deliver what your customer wants. This will put your organization in offering valuable and high-quality products that will always meet the expectations and needs of the customers. It will help you earn a return on investment as quickly as possible.

One thing that should be kept in mind while adopting the agile policy is costs. There's no denying that transforming to an agile policy can be indeed a very hard method to follow. If you're planning to adopt the agile policy, you have to engage the right team along with the right kind of attitude. You have to break things down so that it can be easily achievable. The ambitions should be kept realistic and if you can respond to the feedback, you will be able to reap its rewards.

The thing that should be kept in mind that you have to tailor your agile policy according to the needs of your product or business. You have to use the methods that are right for your business. You need to be true to the context, content, and spirit of the process you're using. In case you're just starting out, it's always better to learn the methods first and then understand them deeply. When you'll gather the full understanding you can then apply the policy. Over time, your team will be able to govern themselves and figure out the best policies for your business as a whole.

The Scope of Agile Project Management

In an agile project, the whole team is responsible for its management. Therefore, the project manager will have the same responsibilities as the other people in the project. This will make sure that there is no such delay when it comes to the decision making of the management and thus things can progress at a much faster rate as well.

The function of the Agile Project Management should be able to demonstrate the skills and leadership in motivating others. This will help in retaining the spirit among all the team members and therefore allows the whole team to be more disciplined. The project manager is not the head of the management when it comes to Agile Project Management. The function of the project manager allows the resources and activities to be coordinated and facilitated in such a way that software development could be done speedily while still maintaining the standard quality.

The Principles Agile Project Management

There are currently twelve key principles in the Agile Project Management guide. They are as follows:

- The highest priority should always be customer satisfaction and it should be achieved with the help of continuous and rapid delivery of products.

- At any stage of the process, any kind of changing environments can be used, which will help the customer obtain various competitive advantages, without a doubt.

- The service or the product should always be delivered at a very high frequency.

- Developers and stakeholders combine and collaborate on a regular basis. Stakeholders include employees, the government, the shareholders and so on.

- In order to achieve project outcomes that are optimal, all the stakeholders along with the team members should keep themselves motivated at all times. Teams will be provided with the necessary support and tools to finally complete the project goals.

- It's always deemed that face-to-face interactions are the most effective and efficient form of communication in order to make a project successful.

- Agile processes are used to maintain sustainable development. On the other hand, developers and stakeholders will be able to maintain a continuous and constant pace.

- With the help of continuous focus on proper design and technical excellence, agility can easily be enhanced within the team members.

- One of the essential elements of agile project management is simplicity.

- The best designs and architectures are developed by only those teams who are self-organized and are able to meet the requirements.

- With the help of fine-tuning behavior, efficiency can be improved at regular intervals.

The Benefits of Agile

As it has been already discussed earlier, agile was mainly developed for the software industry, so that the development process can be improved and streamlined. This was made to rapidly adjust and identify the defects and issues so that those issues can be sorted out easily and quickly. It will provide a way for the developers and the team members to offer a better product in a process that is much faster, with the help of interactive, shorter sprints.

In the 21st century with its digital transformation, there are many companies that are migrating to a workplace that is digital as well. Therefore, agile is the perfect way for organizations to change and transform the way they handle the projects and thereby operate as a whole as well. With the help of agile, there will be an alignment of the company-wide methods and processes.

The following are some of the benefits of agile:

- It helps in increased productivity.

- It helps in improved flexibility.

- It helps in better transparency among team members.

- With the help of agile, higher quality of deliverables can be obtained.

- There will be a decreased risk of any missed objectives.

- The satisfaction and engagement with the stakeholders will be increased as a result.

The Merits (Advantages) Of Agile Project Management

The field of project management, agile provides various benefits to the sponsors, project teams, customers and project leaders. They are as follows:

- The solutions to a given problem will be deployed very rapidly.

- Resources will be minimized so that waste could be reduced.

- There will be increased adaptability and flexibility to incoming change.

- Efforts will be made in a more focused manner so that success could be increased.

- The overall turnaround times will fast.

- Defects and issues will be detected faster and swifter.

- The overall development process can be optimized.

- The framework policy can be made lightweight.

- There will be optimal control over the on-going project.

- Focus power will be increased on what the customer wants and their needs.

- There will be an improved frequency between feedback and collaboration.

Understanding the Principles of Agile

There are currently twelve principles of Agile, which were added after the Agile Manifesto was created. The principles were put into place in order to guide and help teams transition into the philosophy of agile and check whether the practices that are being followed are in line with the culture of agile as well.

The best way to organize those twelve principles would be to put them in their distinctive groups:

- Teamwork

- Customer Satisfaction

- Quality

- Project Management

The following is an in-depth discussion of the twelve principles of Agile.

1. Continuous and Early Delivery of Valuable Software

Products are developed with the help of someone else's money and time so that they can help them simplify their lives in a better manner. If the wait is too long for a product, then the product might not be able to satisfy the customer. In 2019, this is truer than ever before. It's not only fantastic to enjoy valuable feedback at the start but to also have it on a regular basis.

Every delivery throughout the lifecycle of the software or product will add value to the customer. By shortening the time from reporting to the customer, to documenting the project and therefore getting feedback - the real goal of the project can be focused upon. Therefore, you will provide the customer with what they want as per the changing goals and not what you had originally planned.

2. Embracing Change

In the current world, technology is changing at a rapid pace. Therefore, nobody can know or predict the requirements of the software or product that will be released three years later. Also, it should be kept in mind that businesses do not like spending money on a product that will be outdated shortly down the line or worse no longer relevant at all. If you can welcome change to your project, it will prove to be helpful to the customer. This is because the product will be able to meet the latest and current demands of the customer and not of the previous generation or year.

The world has been changing constantly for over a decade. When there is a change in society, the market also changes, which allows organizations and people to change too. Therefore, instead of trying to stop down the process or slowing it down, you need to use the same to your customer's advantage. It's always better to implement the change when the customer wants it and not wait for the next iteration. This will help you get the results instantly. With the help of agile philosophy, you can always stay nimble on your feet without having to constantly reinvent the wheel.

3. Delivery Should Be Frequent

Even though the third principle may sound almost similar to the first one, it differs in its inner meaning. The first principle points out that valuable software should be delivered at an early stage. The third principle goes into a lot more detail and explains the meaning of delivering the software on a continuous basis.

The third principle suggests that you should be always releasing new versions of your product or software within a very short span. With the help of smaller releases, bugs will be fewer as well.

With the help of more frequent releases, there will be more frequent feedback from your customers. This is essential because if you get feedback months later, you have to do a lot of work to fix those bugs and will, therefore, get tiresome too. This principle has become prominent over the years and releasing new software versions over a couple of months isn't agile anymore. The industry has now evolved to have more weekly and daily releases.

4. Developers and Business Together

It's not a new fact but the product developers are always shielded from the technical areas of the business. This is why analysts are put between the businessmen and developers so that the language could be translated from the mouth of businessmen into a language that the developers can understand. With the help of the agile principle, those barriers should be removed. This will help in improving mutual understanding.

There's no denying that any extra step in communication will make the process ineffective. Therefore, analysts acting as a middleman will not be the clear representation of what the business people have to say. Some of the data will get lost in translation. But if you can allow the business people and developers to work together, the issue can be easily mitigated. In the real world as well, teams should work together unitedly. Getting feedback on a regular basis and catching the misunderstandings at the earlier stage will help in achieving a successful result.

5. Individuals Will Be Motivated

A team following agile principles will be responsible for developing quality products. And for this to happen, you need to trust your developers. With the right amount of coaching, tools, and environment - your developers will be motivated in the right manner and will be able to do their job in the most professional way possible.

You cannot make your project a success if you try to build your project around demotivated developers and there is no trust in between. Also, you might end up losing your best developers too. In simple words, you need to stop micromanaging your developers. They will eventually lose morale and you will not be able to get the best productive work from them. You need to step-in when needed and step-out when not.

6. Adopt Face-To-Face Conversation Whenever Possible

With the help of technology, there are a number of ways by which humans can interact with others. But there's no doubt that none of those methods is as effective as face-to-face communication. Human brains interpret all kinds of signals and not just the other person's sound or talking. Facial expressions do matter as well as body language too. Also, there is less chance of misunderstanding to happen with this kind of method.

From the year 2001 to the year 2019, the way we work has changed in a drastic manner. There are corporations that have employees working remotely, including in other time zones as well. There are apps like Slack that create a great way to communicate easily between the product developers. Services like Hangouts and Skype will allow in better face-to-face talks remotely. Still, none of them will be the same as talking to the person as in real-life. Still, there are some teams across the globe who are proving to be successful without having to meet the other people in the team, in real-lie.

7. Software Should Have a Working Demo

It's not surprising to say that software project does take a lot of time to complete. Therefore, businesses have to be very rational when measuring the time it will take to complete. With the help of this agile principle, you will come to know that the best way to measure progress is to have a demo of the product or software, either in the pre-alpha or alpha stage. There's no point in beautiful drawings and graphics, completed models or even analysis that has been done recently - if all those features are not converted into a software having a working model. There's no value for the customer if you haven't used a small part of that planning into something usable for the end-user.

If a product hasn't been shipped or not yet finished working upon it, then no such progress is made. Any software that is unreleased is extra inventory. And to maintain that inventory, you need to spend a piece of income or monetary value.

8. Promotion of Sustainability

In this principle, the consistency of the overall delivery team is mainly emphasized. The whole team should be able to maintain their work ethic over the course of the project duration and should not burn out after a short period.

When developers work over a long time on a specific project, there will be times when the whole team will face the burn-out symptoms and it's quite unavoidable as well. But, still, you have to make sure that you don't overwork your team because the quality of the project will then take a substantial hit in the process. Make sure you get a good team and not let them work overtime, otherwise you can put your whole project in danger.

9. Excellence in Technicality

There are many businesses out there who like to deliver a product in a particular time frame rather than focusing on a good technical design. While that may not be a bad thing, because the customer will not care about the technical design and it will not bring money for the business as well. But, if teams start neglecting good technical designs, then their time and speed will start to slow down. The team will lose the agility and the capability to provide a reaction to the changing market.

When a project is small, then it can make sense to work on a project without having an eye for a good technical design. But if the project is large enough, then paying attention to the technical qualities will pay off in the long-run. It should be kept in mind that this principle doesn't tell you to have a design before the code gets written or the product gets manufactured. Design can easily evolve with the product or software itself. The developers will also need to be responsible and have the time to implement the same too.

10. The Simplicity

Simplification of the project process is very necessary because you cannot maximize your work in several areas. You have to remove the procedures that you think are irrelevant. You have to move towards automation and therefore use the existing resources instead of developing your own. It will help you save money and time, giving you the opportunity to focus on providing more value to the customer.

In every organization, simplification is an on-going work that the company needs to invest in. Keeping things simple is a great way to make your process more streamlined.

11. Teams Should Be Self-Organized

This principle can be termed as the combination of all the previous principles. If you want the developers and the business people to communicate with each other easily on a regular basis, in an effective manner, then only you will be able to measure the progress. For measuring the progress, you also need working software and you need to work with individuals who are motivated enough. Then only you can get the resultant quality product or software.

Therefore, all the above procedures should be self-organized by the team members themselves. The team members should gather their requirements by communicating in the right way with the business people, organize their work, develop quality products and so on. This will help in obtaining better end results because the developers themselves will start to know the value of the product. An agile team of individuals should be able to handle more responsibility than just developing the product or writing the code.

12. React Accordingly

One of the major benefits of putting together a well-rounded team is that the developers will reflect and tweak things during the course of the project. The team should not blindly follow any particular protocol and the project should be adjusted when necessary. You don't want your team to be complacent. You need an evolving group of developers who are constantly engaged and are high on productivity.

No team in the world can be run in the perfect way. An agile team can easily identify the issues, along with having respect for each other's work and then promote action to improve the process too. Successful businesses are built by teams who don't accept their status-quo and they work towards improving the situation.

The Benefits of Agile Project Management

There are numerous benefits that agile project management provides to project teams, organizations as well as products. The following are some of the most prominent ones:

1. The Efficiency

There's no doubt that with the help of agile, teams can be made more efficient. Teams that adopt the agile culture, work in a very collaborative manner and therefore, the efficiency of one person creates a ripple effect on the others. Everyone in the team will accept their respective roles which will allow each person to focus directly on the important tasks.

When an agile team works together, the characteristics of the team become interconnected. This is because of the collaboration, efficiency, and predictability of every person, which helps in creating holistic habits, thereby developing an agile formula.

2. The Product Quality

When it comes to the development in an agile environment, the main testing of the product is done inside a culture having collaborative efforts, so that the final product can be delivered at an ideal state. With the help of this measure, the product developers can make changes to the product if needed and the team will also be aware of the potential issues, which need to be fixed. The Scrum Master will take care of the following key points in order to maintain continuous development:

- Automated testing tools are being generally used.
- In order to make the team acquire the knowledge and features of the product, various elaborating and explaining methods are required.
- Regular testing, as well as continuous integration, is put in the process of development for the product, so that any issues which may pop-up, can be dealt with beforehand.
- The scrum team will be able to achieve maximum efficiency with the help of sprint retrospectives.
- The product development is done in rapid and incremental cycles so that each version's release will depend on the functionality of the previous version. All the versions will be tested rigorously in order to ensure that the quality that is held, is at maximum levels.

- Using a proactive approach in order to prevent any major problems with the product in the future.

- Sustainable development, technology, and good design must be taken into account for product development.

- The work should be completed with these four keywords in mind - integrated, developed, documented and tested.

3. The Predictability of the Project

When companies develop a product, they first calculate the overall value of the project. This value is calculated on the terms of costs versus the overall return on investment or ROI. Therefore, if the ROI exceeds the overall cost to develop the project, then only it is decided to take the project in a positive direction. But if the ROI of the project remains unknown to the company, as can be said with various projects today, the result prediction of the project becomes almost close to being impossible for the company to know.

Thus, this is the singular reason why projects need the help of predictability. With the help of the agile procedures, the team that is working on the project can spend more time on the front end, to make sure that the effort will be worth it or not. By using agile procedures, the team will be able to predict whether the project needs to be continued with or put to an ultimate end. There are numerous tools available in agile project management that can help the team to improve the predictability:

- In order to make sure that the project cost is controlled, the same allocation for the development team and complimentary sprint length should be maintained, so that the team will know about the costs regarding each sprint length.

- Timelines and budgets can easily be predicted with the help of an individual development team having a calculated speed. Other aspects of the product such as backlogs, releases, and other requirements can also be predicted too.

- The daily performance of the project team can be predicted with the help of charts containing sprint breakdowns, scrum meetings held on a daily basis and also task boards as well.

4. The Overall Adaptability of the Team

It's not possible for project managers to look into the future, but with the help of their guidance, at every step of building the project, such an ability could prove to be very crucial. This will help the team to adapt to changes whenever there is a requirement. The cornerstone of agile project management is the ability to adapt and therefore adopt the methods of agile in the work processes.

The team will be able to meet the demands of the customer, without even overspending, if they can become efficient at their work. This method will not only make the client happy but also make the teams that are working on the project become much more quality-oriented towards their job. They'll start to know the project will be the result of their skills and effort.

5. The Return on Investment is Faster

It can be said that the development of agile is iterative, which means that the features of the product are delivered at an incremental rate. This gives an advantage in the overall development process. Customer requirements can be understood easily and products can be delivered at a faster rate, which will modify the further work laid out by the development team. The following advantages can be observed from such procedure:

- The advantage of being the first mover in the market.

- The development is done at an early and fast rate.

- The product will be ready to be marketed.

- By eliminating the long development cycles, the company will have to deal with fewer problems, especially in fast-moving markets.

- Fast product releases will be able to gauge the overall customer reaction and therefore the plan should be made to alter according to the demands so that you can keep ahead of the competition.

- It helps in building better value inside the business. Since the client (or the customer) determines the main priority of the features, the team will be able to know and understand the demand and thus provide the features in the same valuable order as well.

6. Customer Satisfaction

With the help of agile, project team and managers can easily satisfy customers with the following procedures:

- The customer is kept engaged and involved throughout the entire course of the project.

- The customer needs and the requirements of the product need to be handled by the team lead, who is an expert on the product features.

- The backlog of the product must be kept updated and also should be prioritized, in order to make changes in a quicker fashion.

- The working functionality of the product must be demonstrated to the customers in each sprint review.

- The products must be delivered often and quicker to the market with every version of the product.

- Self-funded projects should be processed along with their potential.

7. The Risks Are Reduced

With the help of agile procedures and methods, the chances of project failures are easily eliminated with the help of the following procedures:

- With the help of the methods for agile, you will be able to eliminate the chances for any failure.

- Plan to have a working product, from the first day of working on the project, so that the process could be a success.

- The time between the initial investment and application of a certain approach should be very less because it will help to understand beforehand whether that certain procedure is deemed to work or not.

- The revenue should be generated at an early stage so that the project could be self-funded and the company will have to pay very little costs on an upfront basis.

- With the help of agile methods, the freedom to implement new changes will be provided. Therefore, due to the increase in the number of updates, the overall cost to implement changes will be lower too.

- The client's needs and desires will be catered to throughout the whole development process. This will help in delivering real value to the customers and not just useless features that the customer will not be using anyway. This will also give the project the opportunity to be beta tested by the customers so that each version of the product can receive valuable feedback much earlier in the project life cycle. This will give the development team the need to make changes if required.

8. Team Morale Will Increase

When you're part of a team that is always self-managing, then it will help you to be more knowledgeable and also innovative for the overall expertise. When there is a scrum master working inside the project team, it will shield the team from any external interference and also remove any impediments as well. With the help of cross-functionality, the team members in the development category can be able to grow and learn new skills and also by teaching each other too.

9. The Ownership and Collaboration Will Increase

The scrum master, along with the product owner and the project team will be closely working on the project on a daily basis. With the help of scrum meetings on a daily basis, the development team will be able to organize the work that is to be completed combined with the plans for future work to be done, besides the difficulties that are to be ironed out. The team can discuss the project directly with the stakeholders during sprint reviews so that the progress could be well documented.

10. The Team Structure Can Be Customized

With the help of self-management, the decisions that would most likely be taken by the company or the business manager will now be in the hands of the scrum master or the project lead. Due to the small size of the development team, which mainly consists of five to ten people - an agile project can have more than one team working on a project. With the help of limited size and self-management, these agile driven projects can easily provide the opportunity to customize the work environment and also the team structure as well.

11. The Use of Relevant Metrics

In agile projects, relevant metrics are used to estimate the costs, time, measuring the performance of the project, making decisions based on the project and so on. Therefore, with the help of relevant metric accurate information can be easily obtained, as compared to traditional projects. The following methods are used to provide the metrics calculation:

- The comparison between the value and cost of future development, which will help the team to either end the project there or just deploy more capital on the project.

- The chart for doing sprints should be updated on a daily basis to know the progress of the team with the iteration of the sprint.

- As the project team slowly learns about the project, the overall estimated time, effort and cost can be redefined as per the requirements.

- The use of relative estimates should be promoted rather than using days or hours. Furthermore, the effort of the development team should be in correlation with the team's capabilities and knowledge.

- The performance and the capabilities of the development team should be able to dictate the budget and the project timeline.

- With the help of the project team, the overall work requirements on the project will be estimated.

12. The Increase in Visible Performance and Control of the Project

When it comes to visible performance, every team member working on the project will have the opportunity to know the progress of the project at any given point in time. Progress can be easily be demonstrated with the help of meetings, reviews, and charts.

Coming to the control of the project, the project lead, along with the owner and the entire team has the power to use their measures for controlling and therefore developing better products as a result. This can only be achieved with the help of projects that follow agile procedures.

13. The Increased Focus on Priorities, Productivity, and Transparency

When working in an agile environment, you have to make various decisions and it will be difficult to keep your focus straight on the end goal. Thus, the team should focus on its backlog and ensure that every work is prioritized to ensure the process is streamlined. Not only that, with the help of agile, your resources will be utilized in a better fashion, so that your team could start their work faster and the productivity is always kept at an all-time high.

Since the work will be segregated into separate iterations, there will always be deadlines and milestones to reach. The developers will always be enticed to move forward and will not be sitting idle - even during the design and discovery procedures.

When talking about transparency, everyone involved in the project including the stakeholders will know the current status and progress. There will also be a clear-cut marker on the person taking the majority of the decisions. This will allow the development team to have faith in the system and see the end result in a better manner - which in turn will encourage them to work quickly and effectively.

The Reasons Why Being Agile Is Better

When you talk about being agile, there are a lot of different methodologies that come together in one place. These methodologies include FDD (Feature Driven Development), Scrum and the likes. All these methodologies are a part of the agile manifesto, which was released in the year 2001. These agile methodologies are always compared to the traditional waterfall model in the world of software development. But it has been proven time and time again that agile methods will always trump the traditional processes.

In agile methodologies, an incremental approach is always taken where a sample prototype of the main product is first discussed with the client (or the customer). The sample will help the customer understand the main aspects of the product, along with the requirements as well. Then taking the requirements in mind, the subsequent prototypes are therefore released. These later prototypes reflect the changes that the previous prototypes needed. Such incremental changes will continue to happen until the customer is fully satisfied with the product. This will help the project team to deliver better final products to the customers.

The main idea behind this agile development is to maintain the overall quality of the product, throughout its developmental life cycle. When agile methodologies were compared to the traditional waterfall method, the following changes were needed to be made:

- Each part of the development process should be the ultimate result of the previous step.

- Each process should be repeated and always checked for consistency.

- With the help of a single version or iteration, the complete picture of the process cannot be obtained. That's why multiple iterations are needed in a product life cycle.

Why People Like Being Agile?

It has been reported by a recent online survey that agile is currently the most trending and magical formula to make your project a success. The majority of the development teams all around the world are adopting this methodology because of the benefits it brings on the table. It has been found with the help of further research that when agile was first introduced in 2001, the project team members faced many challenges when trying to implement traditional practices.

At the same time, agile had brought a new style of product or software development, which involved better team collaboration and ultimately more focused on the customer. The ideology was an instant hit among the project leads and developers alike. Thus, the adoption of agile methodologies slowly started to happen.

Even though, it's almost two decades agile was introduced, the adoption has only been high in the last five years. The adoption reached its peak around the year 2009 - 2010. The growth of agile was incremental until the year 2008, after which the adoption hugely accelerated, thereby gaining more traction in the market as well.

It has been found that complex projects always benefit from agile methodologies because these projects contain several stages that are interconnected with each other. Therefore, such interconnection means that a certain change in one stage will lead to another change in the next stage. Project leads or managers thereby started using agile procedures in such complex scenarios, so that the adaptability of the project and its developers can be always high.

Another thing that should be kept in mind is that - due to the increase in the use of agile methodologies, the use of traditional methods (like the waterfall procedure) has been on a steady decline. In the waterfall procedure, you will be able to see the sequential flow of events throughout the lifecycle of the product.

Therefore, the different phases of the product life cycle include design, analysis of requirements, testing, implementation, and production and so on. But when you compare the same to agile methodologies, it will instead deliver better adaptability, visibility, value and also accountability as well. These procedures are implemented from the beginning and will, therefore, minimize risks in the long-term.

It's very well-known that when you're working on a product, project plans change on a weekly or daily basis. The waterfall approach with its sequential passage of events will not be able to cope up with the ever-changing pace of the scope of the project. Comparatively, agile project management always deploys a highly adaptable approach along with the development of various frequent iterations of a certain product. Such processes can highly cope up with the required changes and that has been the crucial reason why people like being agile.

The Reasons Why Agile Is Better Than Traditional Approaches

The following are the major reasons why agile methodologies trump traditional methodologies:

1. The Flexibility

When you use traditional methods, you will find that there is very little room for error. Not only that, but you will also have less room to take advantage of various opportunities as well. But when it comes to agile, it uses short-term sprints, along with numerous iterations of the product. This allows the project team to make mistakes and even later recover from those mistakes at a later iteration. There will also be the ability to use the available opportunities for the development of the product so that a better quality product can be delivered.

When it comes to the development of products and software in the 21st century, product life cycles are always going to be short with changing constantly demands. Therefore, being flexible is the only way you can make your project a success. With the help of progress that is measured in real-time, you'll have the ability to update your product with changing demands and requirements.

2. The Collaboration

In any modern-day project management strategies, collaboration is one of the most essential components. In any industry you look into, collaboration is an essential element to a project's success. That's why the methodologies of agile are the most effective procedures for any company to implement and thereby foster collaboration.

Whether it's during the planning phase or during meetings, agile always encourages collaboration. Such a step leads to the creation of an effective, enjoyable and efficient workplace, which generates not only value but also individual ideas and strength.

3. The Transparency

Feedback from the stakeholders on a consistent basis is very essential when it comes to the development of the product, as per the methodologies of agile. With the help of this ability, user requirements will be passed onto the developers. Throughout the process, tasks have the ability to change, thereby capitalizing on the best features and eliminating the worst ones. With the help of this feedback, the collaboration between team members will also be boosted.

4. The Focus on Results

There's no doubt that the goal of every team that is handling the development of a product, is to be driven by value and also be result-oriented as well. With the help of agile procedures, each achievement is recorded which determines the effectiveness of each sprint, rather than just focusing on the final result. Such processes will encourage continuous adjustments and improvements, not only in the current project but later projects too.

5. The Speed of Delivery

It has been reported by research that almost 80 percent of the companies who are market leaders today, was the first to reach that specific market. With the help of agile methodologies which include delivery of each iteration of the product at regular intervals, early and regular release of the product is promoted. If companies want, they can also maintain their products in perpetual beta version stage as well, like Google did years back with the Chrome Web Browser.

6. The Management of Risk

Due to the small and incremental approach of the agile methodology, the product owner, the team and the team lead will be able to identify any issues at an early stage and therefore, make it easier to respond to change as well. With the help of transparency in agile processes, required business decisions can be taken at the most effective time frames, so that there is time to deal with the difference in the outcome.

7. The Enjoyment

Due to the necessary collaboration, involvement, and cooperation, the development teams following agile procedures will experience the most enjoyment when working at their workplace. Without talking about specifications, requirements will be discussed inside workshops. In place of status reports, there will be a task-board containing the progress of the project. The team will be empowered to make their own decisions and discuss what is right or wrong for the product, instead of investing in management committees and project plans that are lengthy.

All these processes together make the approach much more rewarding for all the developers working together. High performance, well-motivated teams are created via this method only.

8. The Manufacturing of the Right Product

The main idea behind being agile is to always evolve and emerge - thereby having the ability to embrace any change that comes your way. This encourages the team to always build the right products for the customer. Traditional methods can help you deliver successful IT products, which may or may not suit the expectations of the customers. But when it comes to agile development, the customer is always kept at the front of the seat, so that the entire emphasis is on building the right product that will meet the expectations of the customers.

9. The Less Need for Rework

The use of agile methodologies always results in less rework on projects, as the main issues and required changes are already identified at the early stages. Comparatively, when it comes to traditional methods, there is a very possibility for rework to happen - either after the delivery of the product or on completion of a certain milestone.

10. The Creation of Value

In traditional approaches, delivery of value always comes at the end of the entire development process. In any case, if the project costs exceed the overall budget, which can be very likely in the case of IT contracts, there will no money or time left to deliver value to the customer with the help of the product. This makes traditional methods highly vulnerable to any changes in the overall budget. Comparatively, agile methodologies allow for any timely course of action and are therefore show greater adaptability.

11. The Product is delivered at an Optimum State

In an agile work environment, the testing phase always happens during the first sprint. This is to ensure that the product can be delivered in the best way possible. It helps the project lead or manager along with the development team to tweak for any changes that might be required. The same when compared to traditional methods, there's no concept of iterative testing. Thus, it makes traditional methodology-led projects much more prone to failures.

What Are The Main Challenges Of Using Agile Project Management?

Even though there are numerous benefits of implementing Agile Project Management, there are also some challenges that you could face when such implementation takes place as well. These challenges will prevent your development team from scaling in the most successful way possible to the enterprise level.

It has been discovered with the help of developmental studies that the following barriers can be faced by both small and large companies irrespective of their current stance in the industry.

1. The Behavioral Changes

It should come as no surprise that changing how you work can indeed be very difficult. The culture and habits of a massive company are deeply ingrained in its culture as well as its employees too. There's no doubt that human beings do not like to change and when the same developers are confronted with the Agile Project Management transformation, they will always resist the change.

If you accept the change, then it means that the process you're following currently might not be the best or even worse as well. It can easily challenge your values in the long-term. Unless there is a fantastic or extraordinary reason to switch, you'll most likely follow the old processes and behaviors.

2. The Lack of Skilled Product Owners

For many decades in the past, the BRD or the Business Requirements Document has been used. The document may have its shortcomings, but it's still much more familiar to most product owners out there. Those who are mostly involved in such requirements include Business Analysts or BAs and the main stakeholders of the business. They are very new to the concept of Agile. These product owners fail to understand the success behind listening to customers and always hesitate to give up their well-known BRD process to something that is substantially more impactful.

Product owners hesitate to go the extra mile for product development because they view their job merely as a contract with the IT department. Moreover, they fear of trying something new and exciting because they are not skilled enough to handle a new procedure or method like agile.

Nowadays, the development teams who follow the principles of agile and agile project management always use an ALM or Application Lifecycle Management tool. Whereas on the other hand, product owners still continue to use Microsoft Excel or Microsoft Word in order to maintain their product requirements. The disparity in the use of technology and talent inside the same organization can easily lead to decreased collaboration and will ultimately affect the implementation of the policies of agile project management.

3. The Lack of Cross-Functional Teams

In the Agile Manifesto, the main language that has been used to frame the principles, have always referred to the technical members of the product development team as 'developers'. This has led to the understanding that agile principles can only be applied to software development. But it should be kept in mind that the word 'developers' has a massive inner meaning than just employees who like to program or code. In this case, 'developers' mean any kind of product developers who are responsible for delivering a product.

It has been found out through Scrum Guide that cross-functional teams are those teams who are always organized for delivering better customer value and have the perfect competency to fulfill their work without depending upon others. These teams maximize their opportunities for accepting feedback in order to make sure a useful product version is always offered to the customer.

But, the sad reality is, most development teams who are not injected with the agile philosophy, do not possess the cross-functionality between them and thus the implementation of agile project management takes a step back. Cross-functionality is a new idea in the current age.

4. The Failure to Communicate

Communication is one of the main challenges faced when trying to implement the values of agile in a traditional working environment. The challenge is multiplied when the same is tried to be implemented with distributed teams. The main reason behind this is because distributed teams are always limited in their channels of communication. Distributed teams, in this case, are meant by developers of a team who are working in segregated areas, i.e. not present in a singular area at once.

Therefore, where most traditional team members meet each other face-to-face, distributed teams face each other via either speakerphone or better through apps like Hangouts, Skype and Slack. Communication is more than just saying verbal words - a huge part of communication also depends on the non-verbal part as well.

It has been found that development teams who communicate well with each other get things done faster and more effectively. Even though product owners and stakeholders do not get involved much in the process, it's still a good idea to keep them engaged in the overall status of the project.

5. The Lack of Team Ownership

The main focus of agile is to bring the team members together so that they can take ownership of their work and break free from the notion of being told what to do and what not. So, to make the principles of agile work, the team members should be able to follow and work upon their own decisions without relying on others. To make this a norm, the scrum master or the project manager should be able to encourage the team for better communication and thereby be more open towards each other. This will allow them to be more engaged with each other as well as the project too. Analyzing and coming up with solutions on their own should be the way forward.

The most common problem faced in most organizations is that teams always check with their project leads for instructions or decisions to take. Therefore, to change that perspective with the introduction of agile project management policies will always be an uphill task.

6. The Unpreparedness of the Project Lead (Or the Scrum Master)

In an agile environment, the team lead or project lead becomes the scrum master. The main purpose of the scrum master is to make sure that all barriers are identified and removed, between the development team and the ultimate goal of the project. Therefore, rather than telling the development team what to do and dictate their actions, the ideal scrum master should always make sure the process must go smoothly. If project managers start to interfere including giving instructions and keeping the total control within themselves, then it can be very problematic because they will not have the time to do their main task, i.e. cutting down barriers.

With the help of proper agile methodologies, it can be possible to let the project lead learn about micromanagement and therefore give the team members the power to make their own decisions. This will help the scrum masters to always focus on the most important aspects of their job - which includes mainly looking into the needs of the development team and then forwarding those requirements to the higher management.

7. The Over-Ambitious Syndrome

There are many organizations that want to adopt the methodologies of agile on a large scale, throughout the entire process of the company, without trying to implement it on a per-project basis. If you're attempting to implement the policies on a company-wide scale, then it will never work as its intended. This is because the employees will be new to the process and making them learn a new method will always be complex and difficult.

In order to maintain maximum efficiency, the implementation should be made in small steps. It's better to do a trial run with one or two teams. Once those teams start to take care of everything by themselves, then you can easily go ahead and implement the same to the next teams. With the help of gradual implementation, you will be able to avoid the need to handle multiple problems all at once. Moreover, you will be able to focus on one thing at one time.

Another thing to keep a note of is that, if you follow closely the problems faced by the earlier teams, then it will be easier to solve the same on the subsequent teams. Therefore, the process will be much more streamlined and easy for you to handle the pressure.

If the principles of agile are implemented in the correct way, then you can use these principles to complete your projects in the best manner possible. You will not be able to save money but also your time as well. Still, it should be kept in mind that in order to so, the companies should first understand the main principles of agile and also oversee the challenges the team might be facing as a consequence of these principles. If these challenges can be mitigated, then the productivity of the team will improve in a drastic manner.

The increase in efficiency and productivity will be visible to the eyes of the stakeholders and also the business owners as well. It will allow the development team to increase their trust in the project, thereby improving the overall morale of the team members.

What Are The Reasons Why Agile Project Management Could Fail?

There's no doubt that the methods of agile project management have been gaining popularity for some time now. But even the best policies in the world can fail due to a number of reasons. Therefore, if you want your project team to succeed using agile methodologies, then you need to keep in mind about these following potholes that can render your plans ineffective.

The following factors are some of the reasons why you should always keep an eye out for your agile policies so that you can avoid these loopholes.

- The Lack of Experience

It was reported at the 9th annual State of Agile Survey that almost 44 percent of people who voted in the survey complained about lack of experience, affirming that is one of the key reasons for the failure of agile methodologies. Agile is not only about the way you think, but also what you do and the way you do it as well.

The team members who have the deficiency to apply agile practices that are basic in nature will always run into trouble in the later stages of the project when more complex strategies will be involved. Therefore, it is very important that you invest in solid foundations by training your team members in techniques that are agile related and also perform proper coaching for their best use case scenarios. That's only when your money will be better invested.

- Clashes in Company Philosophies versus the Core Values of Agile

Lack of any support for cultural transition and the differences in company philosophies versus the agile values are two of the most popular reasons why agile methodologies fail so often. Agile policies are all about the way you think and what you do according to that thinking. In case the organization's culture is hostile or ignorant to the values and principles of agile, then the success of the in-house team members following agile policies will be very slim indeed.

It should be kept in mind that agile also impacts organizational values as well, and in order to facilitate that transformation, agile policies should be adopted on a wider spectrum. It will allow you to enjoy more success in the long-term.

- No Support From The Management

Sometimes, when an agile transformation is poorly planned, it reduces the massive enthusiasm of the project team and managers, thereby reducing their morale and working capabilities. If the executive guidance is not strong enough, the management department will feel disjointed from the development team.

When an agile transformation takes place, the executives of an organization need to change their behavior in such a way that it will encourage the project team to live the values they want and also help them to understand and adapt to the changing agile values of the organization.

- The External Pressure to Follow Traditional Procedures

This problem is very common in large-sized enterprises, mainly where teams following both agile and traditional methods, work under the same umbrella department. This means that agile policies have to work in tandem with traditional procedures, as opposed to traditional procedures working in tandem with agile policies.

Thus, agile has to co-exist with traditional methodologies, which will ultimately affect the organization's planning, retrospectives, reviews and also agreement on organizational interfaces that are mutual to each other.

- The Team's Unwillingness to Follow Agile Methodologies

Such situations arise when the members of a certain team continue to identify themselves through the use of a different function. Therefore, this leads to the formation of a strong personality between the team members and therefore affects his or her position at the pecking order as well.

Thus, there is a certain disparity and difference in focus and behavior that develops between the team members, according to their pecking order. Capable coaching and training of the tam by the management executives are required to overcome these differences in ideologies.

- The Training Received By the Team is Insufficient

Training can be broken down into three parts:

- The training was received by no one.
- The training was done selectively.
- The training was not up to the mark.

It's not at all a very good idea to skimp on the overall training, because it can never lead to a successful organization. You have to make sure that all your efforts in the implementation of agile policies receive training in the best possible manner, including the management executives as well.

- Unreliability of the Team

If you want your agile project to be successful, the members of the whole organization working on it should be on the exact same wavelength as others. If half of your project team members or even your stakeholders do not attend important meetings - the project will simply fail. The best way to avoid this issue to make sure that your team is efficient enough and is dependable on each other to avoid this common problem.

- The Leaders of the Team Are Weak

Before you choose the best scrum master in your agile project team, you have to make sure that the person is a very strong leader and has commendable leadership qualities as well. But, not every person out there has the perfect leadership qualities to make the team work together in unity.

When leaders are weak, the same precedent will be set before the team members too. The scrum master or the project lead should have the capabilities to oversee, lead and also perform any decision or action that is to be undertaken.

- Lack of Any Communication with the Stakeholders

Any deterioration or lack of communication between the stakeholders can easily be the downfall of any agile related project. There can be times when stakeholders will not be fully transparent about their expectations from the team members as well as the project offerings. You have to set up good communication channels with your organization to ensure that such things do not happen and stakeholders are fully able to express and present their necessities to the agile project team members.

- Specifications of the Project is Incomplete

Sometimes projects can fail due to the requirements of the project not being defined in the right manner. Agile projects always focus on the important deliverables and actions of a project and then deals with any possibilities that may come up during the overall implementation of the process. Having a project with requirements that are almost incomplete will prevent the project to go into the actionable mode - which is very important to make the project a success.

- Implementation of the Retrospective is Not Effective

One of the main goals of carrying out agile projects is to perform retrospectives and discuss the same with your team members. A retrospective is all about learning from the process - the positives and negatives. It will help you to know how well the team is performing and how the performance could be made better as well. If you're not carrying out retrospectives, then your team will not come to know about their faults.

It will be much more difficult to know the current stance of each person and collaborative efforts within each other will be difficult. Therefore retrospective meetings should be taken at regular intervals.

- Team Is Focused On Success and Not the Art of Learning

One of the huge reasons for the failure of agile projects is the lack of ambition to learn first rather than to succeed at first. Team members become focused too much on project success and forget the opportunities to learn the various values and methods of agile project management. Mistakes should always be seen as a way to improve and learn something new. For example, if a software doesn't work as you would have expected it to be, you have to see it as an opportunity to learn something new rather than seeing it as a failure.

- Lack of a Set of Best Methods in Agile Project Management

When you compare agile with policies such as Six Sigma, it doesn't have it set of best practices or methods that one could follow. Due to this reason, the agile policies of two different organizations may vary hugely. You have to let your team know clearly about your expectations.

If some policies don't work, you need to strike it off the list as fast as you can. And when some policies will work, you have to add to the list. The trial and error method should be used in this case because agile project management doesn't give you the framework of the best procedures or methods.

- Time is Used Inefficiently

It's quite impossible to complete a project successfully without the following time in the right manner. Time management skills are very important if you want to succeed in any given field or industry. If you spend too much time on developing a single feature, the other features of the project will suffer. Similarly, spending less than the required time will make the feature half-baked or buggy. Time management should not be underestimated and with agile methods, you always need to keep on your toes to achieve the best results.

Agile Environment and Behavior in Action

An agile environment can be defined as an organization or a company that supports and creates the implementation of Agile Project Management. This translates to the organization culture encouraging project teams to adopt the agile principles and also its values.

Companies having an agile environment generally promote and accept innovation, change and process improvement too. These organizations understand and know the various different frameworks of the agile environment and therefore support such practices of agile policies as well. Some of these policies include working in a collaborative manner and doing short or long sprints. Engaged customers and employees are more important to them than just following documented contracts and processes.

Main Characteristics of an Agile Environment

- Leadership in an agile environment should be all about serving a purpose and nothing else.
- Always plan and try to make improvements on a continuous basis and it should be a natural part of the company's culture.

- Results and relationships between the management and the project developers should bring joy into the whole working process.

- Deliveries of the product or software should be made on a frequent basis so that shorter feedback loops can be implemented, which can lead to better quality products and engagement with the customer.

- The value of the business should be delivered by cross-functional, small, self-organizing and co-located teams.

- The members of the team should be stable enough to increase their performance in the long run.

- Decision making should be made decentralized and the same should be supported by the management as well.

- Face-to-face interaction should replace any kind of traditional documentation or other communication methods.

- The focus should be given on obtaining full transparency.

- All the big sized projects should be delivered with the help of a small independent project, which will add increased value to the overall procedure.

The Tools That Are Used In Agile Environment

- Active Collab - It's a tool that is used by small businesses and it quite affordable as well. The tool is very easy to use, and using this to assist software development needs very little training and will still provide brilliant support.

- Agile For Scrum - With the help of this tool, the stakeholders and the product owners get updated instantly with the progress of the project. Some of the features supported by this tool include reports and charts, which are indeed a great option for data mining.

- Agile + Atlassian Jira - This can be termed as a very powerful tool used for management purposes. The tool improves the development purposes by mainly incorporating Kanban, Scrum and also workflows that are customizable.

- Pivotal Tracker – This tool is generally used for methodology, which is mainly geared towards projects that are built for smartphones (and tablets). Even though the toll needs good knowledge for it to be operated, it becomes very user-friendly at a later stage when the user passes the small orientation period.

- Prefix - This is a free tool developed for providing an instant feedback loop for identifying bugs and fixing them before the product or software is finally deployed.

Creating an Agile Environment and Structuring a Team

As agile policies are becoming more and more widespread, there is an increasing number of organizations who are jumping on the agile bandwagon in a heartbeat. The main reason behind this switch is to enjoy the benefits of increased quick turnaround, flexibility and also face lower risks as well.

Making the shift to agile is not only about implementing a new set of processes and templates, but also changing the overall culture and attitudes of the development team, including the supporting organization too. The deeply embedded habits and working practices should be altered.

Steps To Structure a Team and Create an Agile Environment

- Planning In Iterations or Stages

Instead of delivering the product all at once, the project should be split into a set of logical steps - on the completion of each of these steps, a tangible out or the deliverable will be obtained. In this way, you will be building your product or software in a gradual fashion instead of using an approach that will be risky. Each stage should deliver something meaningful to the end-user and that is what matters in this case.

- Keep The Aspect Of Human Beings In Mind

When the planning stage will start, you should make an effort to include your user community and the development team in the mix as well. You have to discuss the benefits of agile and also promote the reasons why it'd be a good initiative to kick-start a new revolution in product development. If you're planning to motivate your team, there's no better way to do that than creating an agile environment.

- Use The Eighty-Twenty Rule

The 80:20 rule states that the development team of a product should focus on the 20 percent of features that will be responsible for delivering 80 percent benefits to the customer. You have to do the same at every stage of your iteration process and therefore know the features that are worthy of being worked and concentrated upon. Another rule that you should follow is to deliver always the risky features at first and then follow up with the non-risky or essential features at later stages.

- Creating a Prototype

If you want your team to work in an iterative manner, you need to always practice building prototypes for your product. Creating a prototype will help you gain early feedback from the community and also reduce the project risks too. It will be a great and tangible way of letting the audience know what the final product is going to be and create a unified vision around your development team.

- Improve Collaboration and Continue To Review and Adjust

In an agile project, user involvement and collaboration play a huge role because the whole team has to play its part in shaping the entire project. Also, continuous learning, reviewing and adjusting should a part of the process from the beginning. At each stage, the review process should tell about the methods that are working well and those that aren't. Agile is all about efficiently and rapidly adapting to change.

Methods to Create Agile Rules and Values

Agile rules and values are not at all complex to implement and use, but they very much require a very deep understanding of the reason you wanted them in the first place. The process requires a shift in mindset before you can let your organization use the necessary tools to improve productivity.

Things to Do For the Creation of Agile Rules and Values

- Clarify The Organization's Vision

An inspiring, clear and shared vision will allow the development team to improve their motivational goals and thus get involved in the practice of agile rules and values. In order to make sure that the project of the organization is a success, the vision should be combined with a well-constructed, strong and embodies cultural identity to give it all its power.

In a fast, uncertain and complex environment practicing agile, being cooperative and having the agility should be the two essential ingredients. You have to ensure that the company's vision is clear to measure the predicted results and that everyone in the team should come to know about it.

- Creating a Fresh Culture

In an agile culture, employees are always valued more and you will enjoy understanding and mutual respect from one another. You have to provide each other with the opportunity to express their true potential. With the help of this new learning culture, you will be able to motivate your team in the long-run. The current generation of employees is always eager for new experiences and innovation, which is a brilliant advantage to have.

Such implementation will help in contributing towards the personal development of the employees which in turn will approve the organization's growth. There would be greater room to include motivation, engagement, and standards for developing a product.

- Fostering Self-Organization

Without the required support, agile teams cannot be self-organized. The self-organized team doesn't come from just having decision making powers. Self-organization is all about the team knowing its members and also each person's skill set. The team should know their level of maturity, their ambition and the things they need to do in order to achieve that ambition in a successful manner.

If you have a self-organization team in your company, it can work as a great performance booster for the other development teams in the same company. It's also a structured and broad way of empowering employees in your company.

- Helps Everyone in Embodying Their New Roles

The methods of agile depend upon various specific roles in order to ensure maximum performance and balance with the development teams. Therefore, setting up those roles as per their mentioned designs are necessary in order to create agile rules and values. Some of the major roles include the product owner, the manager (acting as an intermediary between the scrum master and the product owner), the scrum master (or the project lead) and finally the development team.

How to Use Agile Project Management Effectively?

Agile project management is all about faster development and more frequent releases relating to the product versions so that issues can easily be ironed out and customer satisfaction will always be high. But, it should be kept in mind that agile has its own quirks.

Even though the agile procedure is used by various trillion-dollar companies in the world, you have to know in-depth about the method before planning to dive in. The following guide will help you know the ways by which you can use the agile project management policies in an efficient manner.

Methods to Utilize Agile Project Management on an Effective Basis

1. The Planning of the Project

Just like any other project, before you start, you and your team should be on the same wavelength and understand the end goal of the project. Furthermore, the value of the project in regards to the client and organization along with how the end goal can be achieved should also be understood as well.

You need to develop the scope of the project, but it should be kept in mind that the main purpose of using agile project management is to be able to address all the additions and changes to the overall plans of the project easily. Therefore, the scope of the project should be dynamic and not unchangeable.

2. Time to Hire a Qualified Project Manager

The main job of a project manager is to set up the tasks and goals combined with a timeline for the completion of the task, assigned to the respective project members. They help in evaluating the process and thereby make any necessary adjustments (if needed), to make sure that the project team could achieve the results that are desired.

You can find project managers working in almost every agile industry, particularly in the Information Technology sector and also computer systems and solutions. They are the main reason why activities between different development teams are coordinated, budgets are set and project deadlines are met within the outlined resources.

3. Developing Shared Responsibility or Accountability in the Team

The industry of Information Technology is always full of testers, specialists, developers, and the likes. Even though it can be a great option to have such talented people beside you when working on the project - the same talent can also be a curse for them, especially when they're working in an agile environment. When you start an agile project, it's very important to ask the development team about shared responsibility. Shared responsibility, in this case, means that if a particular developer could not attend his or her work shift, the other developers will be able to nullify the setback effect by accepting the work of the absent developer, equally among them.

It's all about making the calls altogether and thereby acknowledging the same decision as a unified team. The team should be happy about the decision that they've taken and thus have decided to carry the responsibility of the same too. For some developers out there, it can be a major problem while for others it will be a chance to make the project a success. Therefore, it's essential that you get this point across to the members of the project, especially the development team. You can easily challenge the developers are by asking the following questions:

- What will be the action if a person in the project team is slow at his or her work or couldn't attend the working schedule?
- Ways by which such a problem can be avoided.
- Methods by which such an impact could be minimized in the long-term.

The above perspective should be implemented in advance with the project team. You need to generally focus on the areas that your team might face problems. If required, you can also train the required candidates too. The more continuously this process is carried out, the more impact you and your team will start to experience.

4. Setting Up Your Vision With A Mission Strategy

When an agile project is being planned, you always need to define a clear business plan, need or vision, which your project might be addressed towards. You have to answer the reasons why you're going ahead with the project. The core belief of you and your team will help you straighten out your priorities right from the get-go. You can follow the following strategy in order to set up your meaningful vision:

- For - The Target Customer
- Who - The Necessity Of The Project
- The - Includes The Product Name And Also Its Category
- That - The Main Advantages Of The Product And The Reason To Use Or Buy It
- Unlike - The Main Alternative Competitor Product For The Same
- Product - The Final Mission Statement Differentiating The Product From Its Competitors

By following the above method, you can easily adjust this pitch according to your project goals. It will help you define every bit of your procedure. You should ensure that when you'll be making this above pitch - your stakeholders along with your managers, executives, directors, product owners, and the likes should be present. The mission statement is mainly for the upper management, who will be responsible for providing you with the support and necessary monetary investment.

You can decide to do this strategy meeting any time after the project begins to take shape or you can do it on an annual basis too. Make sure the strategy is always valid and any updates (if needed) should be done with the help of periodic meetings.

5. Creation of the Product Roadmap

After your strategy has been validated by the top management of the company, it's time to translate the same insight into a comprehensive roadmap for the product. It will be the high-level view of all your product requirements combined with a loosely adjusted timeframe within which each feature will be developed.

In simpler terms, a roadmap will contain a breakdown of the entire project in hand. It will contain all the features that will be present in the final product. A roadmap is one of the most important parts of the main planning phase. This is because the team will be building these individual features with every sprint they make.

Creating a product backlog in this planning stage is also a necessary move as well. It will contain all the list of features and also the most important deliverables - making up the final product. This backlog will be like the guidebook for your team so that during team sprints, it becomes much easier to refer back and thereby plan ahead.

The loosely adjusted timeframe of the product roadmap is very important because you and your team will not be spending days, weeks or months on the product, but will be using the roadmap to prioritize your goals. Then the estimation of the time that will be taken for each goal will be then used to create the final version of the roadmap. Agile project management is all about theme-based or goal-based roadmap for the product.

Goal-based roadmaps of the product include increasing engagement with the customers, acquiring new users and abolishing any technical debt that might have to do with the project. Features should be derived from the goals themselves and only should be used sparingly. About 3 - 5 percent of features should be used per stage of the goals.

It should be kept in mind that the product roadmap should be created by the product owner, along with the suggestions and recommendations from stakeholders, development teams, marketing and sales teams and so on. Also, the roadmap should be ready before you start planning out your first sprint. Therefore, the motive to create the roadmap should be instantly after the strategic meeting. Ensure to put as much time as possible in the product roadmap until everyone in the team is confident about its success.

6. Chalking Up the Release Plan

After you've got your strategy lined up, the time is now up to set up the tentative timelines. In this stage, a high-level timetable should be announced, which will help in churning out the prototype software faster. Since agile is all about making several releases after the first time, you have to decide and prioritize the features that you may want to launch first. When it comes to traditional project management plans, there is only one date that is used for implementing the features after the whole project has been fully structured and developed. The same cannot be said about agile. In agile project management, products use sprints or shorter development cycles with features being implemented at the end of each sprint or cycle.

The above can be explained by the following example - you start your roadmap in the month of October and you're planning to have an early launch in the month of January and then followed by the later releases in April, July and so on.

The time frame will depend on the work that your team can put up within each sprint and also the overall difficulty of the project too. Each goal will have its work dedicated to them. A regular release should contain about 3 - 5 sprints.

The release plan of a product can be defined as getting your team ready for the work ahead. Everyone related to the project should be present at the release plan, including project managers and stakeholders. This release plan will help you reassess and revisit at following stages of your project.

7. Planning For the Sprints

After you've done with the release planning, the time has come to move the focus from macro to micro perspective. The product owner along with the development team plans their sprints, which can be defined as specific goals or tasks with development cycles that are shorter in nature. When you talk about a sprint, it generally lasts for about one to four weeks at most. The sprints should have the same lengths throughout the life of the project, as it will help in predicting the future work in a precise manner, based on the team's performance in the past.

Before a sprint starts to take its shape to be put into play, the product owner(s) and the stakeholders need a base plan to know the tasks that will be achieved or accomplished in each sprint. The process of achieving the goal along with the complexity of the task is also verified. It's very essential to share the work pressure of the project evenly among its members so that each member will be able to perform their tasks efficiently.

The development team will create a backlog of items that are predicted to be completed within that same sprint cycle. This will help you create a very functional software. Then you can further use any other agile project management procedures to finely tune the procedure. It's always better to visually document your entire workflow in terms of a video or a flowchart so that there are no issues with transparency in the team. The team will experience shared understanding between them and therefore removing any bottlenecks that are being identified.

Since the entire team will be backing the sprints, everyone in the team including the project managers, product owners, and team members should be able to voice their opinions, concerns, and thoughts as well. Also, if you're doing weekly sprints, make sure that you do the planning on the first day of every week, i.e. it can be either Sunday or a working day such as Monday.

8 Perform Meetings on a Daily Basis

You have to ensure that throughout the operations of every sprinting process, there should be no barriers that might be hindering the overall performance of the team. The goal should be to complete the designated targets on or before the due date. This is the reason having daily meetings are very important. Daily meetings will help your team to access and accomplish their tasks in each sprint in the most efficient manner. In case any changes are needed, the same should be discussed in the daily meetings. Each member will talk about the tasks that they have been able to accomplish the day before and also describe the task that will be worked upon on the same day.

A daily meeting should mainly have a maximum duration of 15- 20 minutes. These meetings should not be used for problem-solving sessions or talk about new ideas or designs. The following criteria should be discussed in the daily meetings:

- The work that has been completed yesterday.

- The work that is to be completed today.

- If the work is facing any hindrance from barriers or roadblocks (technical difficulties).

It can be possible that some members of the team might be annoyed with the daily meetings and doing the same thing every day. But, it should be kept in mind that such a step is taken for improving the communication between the project members, which will help in driving the agile project management. Being agile is all about quickly responding and voicing your feedback towards issues so that a better cross-team collaboration could take place.

9. Review for the Completed Sprints

Until this point, if everything has gone according to plans, then you can be sure of obtaining a functional software at the end of your sprint timeline. The time will be to show and also review the work that has been done to all the other members of the project including the stakeholders and product owners. It can be described as an end credit in a movie.

It's recommended to hold at least two meetings for the same purpose. The first should be about the sprint review with the stakeholders for showing the completed product - which will help in keeping the communication channels open with the stakeholders, in the near future. The process should either be performed through a face-to-face chat (which is recommended in case of agile projects) or through a video-conference over the internet via Skype.

The second meeting should consist of a rigorous discussion about the project with the stakeholders and product owner(s). The discussion should include the processes that have gone in the right way for the team, the processes which could have been implemented in a better way, revealing about the complexity of the project (whether the work pressure was high or low) for every member of the team and the results that were gained through sprinting. The main thing to note here is that to ensure that the requirements of the original plan have been met. The product owner will have every right to refuse or even accept the functionalities of a product. This will help in adjusting the next sprint according to the necessary requirements so that further goals can be obtained by the development team. The process of iterations and learning should be continuous which will be reflected in your product as well.

In case your team is new to the concept of agile and its project management policies, then this necessary review meeting should not be skipped. It will help you to understand and even predict the number of tasks or work your team is capable of doing so that you tune the next sprints to be more efficient.

10. Learning through Mistakes and Constant Improvement

If you want the policies of agile project management to work in the best way possible, you need to clearly define the next steps. The later sprints will be determined according to the reports that you obtained from the previous sprint review. Once a sprint has been completed and all the developed features have been shown, it's time to decide on the next goals.

This will be the perfect time to brush up on the mistakes that have been committed before and thereby develop plans to improve upon those mistakes. Learning is a constant phenomenon that should be put to good use.

Make sure you take the time to discuss the merits and demerits of the previous sprint with the project team so that improvements could be suggested. This learning and improvement phase is the general extension of the sprint review. So, it may be possible that the stakeholders might not be interested in the same. But, the entire team except the stakeholders should be present and also giving their own opinions too.

Up to this stage, you will most probably have a prototype functional software that will be possible to ship out to the customers. Doing so will help you get feedback on the same and thereby also plan for new features too. Agile is all about continuous processes - the leaning, building, and shipping.

Your project team will be able to release products effectively and thereby demonstrate the interactive behavior with the users. Rather than working and waiting for a whole year to release your product, you can release it early and thereby adjust your sprints according to the audience's behavior.

The Phases of Agile Project Management

In a world where traditional opinions and structures were more given more preferences, these five agile project management phases were introduced in order to help project teams who were following agile methodologies, thereby allowing them to enjoy the understanding and freedom they want from their project procedures.

The main person behind the development of these five phases is Jim Higsmith, who was also one of the original signers of the Agile Manifesto. These five phases mirror the exact same routine as the original agile policies, which include the following - initiation, planning, managing, controlling and closing phases. The following in-depth explanation will help you understand every stage in greater detail.

The Envision Phase

This phase is made to determine the vision of the product that has been developed or is currently in the process of doing so. It also studies the scope of the project as well and the process by which the team will work together too. It should be kept in mind that the real meaning of the word, 'envision' is quite different from the traditional meaning, i.e. to initiate and plan.

The reason behind this is that - when you envision something, it means that you're ready to accept any change of plans during the course of the project if the original project doesn't work out. It also means that you're not following a strict plan or path that is not dynamic. This phase mainly covers the following three things - Who, What and How.

If you don't have a clear vision, then creating a successful product will not be possible by means. Another thing that should be noted here is that - creating a vision that is compelling enough is already a very challenging task in itself. It not only takes hard work but also the right kind of leadership capabilities.

Since there are various pathways to choose from when creating a strong vision for the future, it can easily become confusing for someone new at this scene. It is thereby very essential to have a competent and effective leader among the whole project team to push the ideas forward and further articulate a new vision for the organization. The main purpose of this phase is to identify clearly the work needs to be done and the method that needs to be allowed to get that task accomplished.

The envision phase should be able to answer the following questions:

- The vision for the customer's product.
- The constraints and scope of the project should be kept in mind.
- The right kind of people to include in the community which is building the project.
- The procedure through which the team will be delivering the project.

When the envision phase starts its cycle, the vision can change itself throughout its course as the project team gathers new data and information about the project. Once the project team gets over this phase, the vision still should be reviewed in a periodical manner to ensure everyone inside the team has a greater understanding of the same.

If you look at the technical side of things, it can be separated into four main steps:

- Scope
- Vision

- Approach

- Community

When a particular vision or scope is being created, the architecture of the project can be used to streamline the overall vision. You can use the product vision box to force your team to work in increased collaboration and focus, thereby leading to better results in the future. Community is all about getting the right kind of people inside your team and the approach will define the result delivery process of the main project.

The Speculative Phase

The word speculation might mean that it involves a lot of risk-taking and reckless thinking. But, in true words, speculation means that it encourages collaboration and brainstorming, mainly based on creative thinking. This allows the team members to envision and thereby explore all the possibilities through which the project should progress.

The speculative phase shouldn't be compared to the planning of the project because speculation sets a direction and a target. At the same time, it also sets a precedent that changes can be expected throughout the course of the project's lifetime. But, when the same is compared to planning, it can be seen that a plan is all about a future result that people want to achieve through the said plan. If you deviate from the planned events, it will be viewed as something negative - whereas, in speculation, the same is viewed generally as a positive move.

In order to determine the course of your action, the information should be examined through speculation. The result of the speculation will create a blueprint, which will be outlining all the required information about the product's specification, risk analysis, architecture of the platform, business constraints, levels of the defect, target schedules and so on.

In this phase, there are two main and crucial components that should be kept in mind - one being short iterations and the other being features. With the help of short iterations, you will be able to accelerate the overall progress of the project. You need to encourage your project team to think in such a way that all the aspects of product development should be done in a limited amount of time. At the same time, the quality assurance team should also try to be more efficient and effective as well, thereby coordinating the tasks of the development team.

When it comes to features, the development of the product should start by creating an extensive list of features that will be added to the product in the future. Before planning for the features, the process should be made understandable and visible to the project team handling the consumer department. Often you will see that development teams will invest their time and money on the project without having a clear understanding of what the customer wants. Therefore, understanding the needs of the customer is the first thing that should be done before chalking out the necessary features.

The following things should be kept in mind during the speculation phase:

- Knowing what the project is and how the features will evolve over time.
- Balancing the act between the adaptation and anticipation of new features for the product.
- Always make sure to focus on the features that will provide the highest value, during the starting phase.
- Always keep in mind the business goals, project ambition and also the expectations of the customers.

- Provide schedule and the necessary budget to the management of the organization.

- As changes will start to occur, you need to make priorities for making trade-offs.

- Always keep in mind about adaptive and alternative actions.

- Activities should be interrelated between different developmental teams.

- Events should be analyzed by keeping a baseline.

The Advance Release Phase

The main job of this phase is to deliver the features of the product. After we've gained an insight on the first two phases of the agile project management - both of which are based largely on projections that are planned, it's time to finally change our stance towards the phase of exploration.

In a project, the main goal of the project manager is to make sure that the team understands the constraints and ambition of the project, so that team interaction could happen efficiently. This will lead to a better process for decision making and making sure that the project doesn't go off-track. The role of the project manager can be explained as below:

- Allowing the team to focus and thereby deliver the required results.

- Taking a group of individuals and mold them into a team.

- Help to develop their capabilities.

- Allowing the team to use the required resources.

- Commanding the overall rhythm of the team.

Therefore, the main aim of the project manager to create teams that have the capability to efficiently explore. It should be kept in mind that experimentation and exploration are the main foundations of product development, which generally involve the risk of failing, making mistakes and then learning from the same. Risks should be taken in such a way that it will not put the organization's actions into jeopardy.

The first objective of the team is to deliver the required objectives which are also facilitated by the management of the organization as well. The main objective of the workload management is to make sure that every member of the team will manage their day-to-day activities in the right manner, which will ultimately deliver the right kind features at the end of its iterations. When it comes to low-cost changes and technical practices, the main aim of the low-cost change is to ensure the cost of any changes in the planning of the project remains the same throughout the lifecycle of the project.

Technical debt is caused when there is a difference between the optimal cost of the plan change and the actual cost of the same. Technical debt happens when changes are done in a hasty manner by the project manager.

The project team should be coached and developed in such a way that helping each other will constantly improve each other's skills and capabilities. Daily meetings are required to help the team members coordinate with each other in the best manner. It will also help the team take various analytical decisions and also interact with the customers so that the requirements of the customers are always kept high on the priority list. Therefore, all of the practices should work in synergy with each other for creating an efficient and effective strategy via an iterative procedure.

The Adapt Phase

This phase mainly focuses on the changes, modifications, and corrections that are done in the lifecycle of a product. The main aim is to explore, speculate and adapt so that you will be able to change your product with every iteration.

Since agile project management mainly consists of exploration, hypothesis testing and also speculation, it's also important for project managers to respond in an effective way after the release has been taken place. It is very necessary to see and notice that how a project will depend on a good understanding, on the basis of the information that is presented, which will provide an insight on the progress of the project combined with the market analysis and also the technical risks as well.

The adaptive phase is designed to see the obtained results through various perspectives, ranging from the customers to the staff that has worked on it. Analyzing will help in focusing on the results that have been obtained versus what was originally planned. It also includes reviewing the results - actual versus the revised ones. The adapt phase will take these changes into consideration and will try to implement them in the next iteration.

There have been many projects in the past which have oscillated in the same way without any signs of growth, due to lack of vision from the project lead. You need to continually use feedback, mainly for adapting your project to the demands of the market. The following things should be kept in mind while doing this:

- Product quality and functionality.

- Performance of the team.

- Status of the project.

This phase should not be termed as a corrective phase because the corrective phase means that the original idea has either made an error or has underperformed, which is not the true scenario in this case. Adaptive phase means the use of structured plans that are exploratory in nature, to aid in the betterment of the project's future.

The following three factors should be remembered when trying to troubleshoot in this specific phase:

- The Value Customers Are Getting From The Project

When it comes to agile projects, changes are always introduced with the help of multiple iterations of a product and therefore the project team should continue to review the value of the product as well. Even though it might seem like a simple task, gaining customer feedback is not an easy process. The value ascertaining procedure is a much more difficult task than measuring the overall cost of the project.

You can use the rankings made by the customer as well as the projected returns on the product as a way to determine the value of the project. The project manager, regardless of the method, should have the urgency to know the project's value.

- The Progression Of The Project At A Satisfactory Pace

Project managers should have the relevant data to answer whether the project is progressing at a satisfactory pace and that success is being achieved on a gradual basis. You can measure the progress in various different ways - with the help of value analysis - which creates the overall value from the product features that are completed. This process is more common with projects that are larger in size and such projects are mainly government-mandated as well.

When we talk about small-sized projects, then if you can create a simple graph containing all the features that have been implemented thus far into the product, then it will serve as an essential way to know the value. Therefore, even though the answer might be very straightforward, the actual answer may be very hard to come by because of the involvement of various factors. Satisfactory performance is not just about following the plan in the right manner but also knowing the related factors too.

- Adaptation of the Project Team in Response to the Changes Demanded by Customers, Management and Technology

As the project will start to evolve over time, the requirements of the project will also continue to change as well. There can be changes in staff or any kind of delay in component might also occur as well. It's very important to reward and appreciate the team members who always respond and adapt to circumstances that are unforeseen - which helps in creating teams that always strive for the best.

If a certain team deviates from the main plan and thereby effectively responds to a competitor product, then the same team should be evaluated for knowing the secrets to their success and not the original failed plan.

The adaptive phase consists of generally a single practice which is then segregated into multiple sub-practices. These sub-practices refer to team review, project, product, adaptive actions, and the likes. For conducting an adaptive action and review session at the end of every iteration, there are two reasons.

The first reason is to learn and reflect and the second reason to change the exploration method or pace with the help of the next iteration. When the reflection period is on-going, user reviews are highly regarded as a way to know the faults with the product and also the way to correct the same too. The adapting phase is indeed one of the most important stages of a project lifecycle because it allows project managers to create a responsive strategy in order to counter the negatives and focus more on the positives so that the product could see a successful ending.

One of the other adaptive strategies is the use of scheduling status, which will be showing all the projected dates for the proposed product. During the planning stage, the team will take care of the amount of time that will be taken for the entire project to complete. It consists of low, high and probable schedules. When a project starts to take shape, there will be uncertainty about the time that will be required to implement each feature, but as soon as the project will be nearing its end, the schedule will become more certain.

The Closing Phase

Every project should have a sweet ending. If you fail to determine the endpoint of a project, then it can easily result in perception issues among all your customers. Often the closing phase of a project is hurriedly done and not enough importance is given since the other essential parts have already been covered. But, that shouldn't be the case.

When resources are scarce, people move onto the next project without taking the required time to close the last project they've worked upon or even receiving/giving credit for the same as well. This can especially be bad for team morals since it's not a functional way to organize a project. Team members will always remain unaware of the project progress.

When a project is to be closed, there are several activities that can be performed. First and foremost should be the celebration.

The celebration will serve two main primary purposes - one being that celebration will provide a sense of closure in terms of the project team and also the project itself. The second being a sense of appreciation for the team members who have worked hard on the project for many weeks and even months. When projects go on for eternity without any sense of closure, it can be pretty disheartening for the team morale.

The second activity that should be carried on is to finalist all the required documents and prepare for the project to be ended. This includes both the financial and administrative reports as well. The third activity that should be kept in mind is to carry out a retrospective of the project, which was already done in a lesser fashion in the iterative process. This retrospective will act as a way to allow the team to learn and thereby pass the judgment to the other members and teams too. It will act as the negatives and positives to build upon your next project.

Thus, in a conclusive manner, it can be said that these five phases in the agile project management are very integral, especially the closing and adaptive phases. These phases are far more than just being a checklist for agile project management. Instead, these phases provide a structural framework for other agile related concepts, ideas, and practices to accommodate.

Each phase shouldn't be separated from one another and should occur strictly after each other. The phases should overlap one-another and also should be revisited when any kind of new information is discovered as well.

The Canon of Agile Methodologies

Agile methodologies can be defined as practices that help in promoting continuous iteration of testing and development throughout the development of the project. These testing and developmental activities are concurrent when compared to traditional waterfall methods and therefore turn out to better measure overall as well.

In this guide, we'll be discussing the most popular agile methodologies that are used nowadays. Each procedure will have its terminology, unique practices, and tactics. Therefore, it's suggested that you study each methodology in the best way possible and thereby plan to implement the same.

Scrum

This method can be characterized as one of the most popular frameworks out of all the agile methods. Scrum is mainly characterized by stages or cycles of development, which are known as 'sprints'. It also leads to an increase in the overall development time for each project as well. Scrum is mainly used for projects that are based on software, but the principles can also be used for content that is business-related too.

Scrum can be defined as a lightweight procedure for following agile methodologies, which can easily be used to manage incremental and iterative projects of various types. Over the years, it has become popular due to its proven productivity, simplicity and also the overall ability to incorporate various practices that are promoted by other agile processes.

In this process, the product owner will work very closely with the team to help in identifying as well as prioritizing the overall functionality of the system, by maintaining a product backlog. The backlog will consist of the list of things that needs to be successfully completed, which includes bug fixes, features, and various requirements that are non-functional in nature, etcetera.

After the main priorities have been established, the teams that are cross-functional in nature will sign-up and estimate the time that will require to complete such required tasks. This will be done by performing successful sprinting on a regular basis, which generally should last a maximum of thirty days. After the product backlog has been fully structured and figured out, no other functionality can be added to it, except by the team itself.

The backlog will again be reprioritized and analyzed after every sprint. This will help in setting up the next deliverables for the subsequent sprint.

Merits

- The innovation of the team is high is because the deadline for each project needs to be met by every programmer.
- Project transparency will be followed by not only the project members but also other employees of the organization involved in the same task.
- Mistakes encountered are fewer in scrum due to the constant focus on overall quality.
- Scrum allows developers to help their priorities to be reorganized so that the sprints which are left out to be completed can get more attention.

Demerits

- Confusion can happen inside the team since the role of each developer is not fully described in the right manner.

- Due to the segmentation of the project, the team can easily lose track of the other parts by focusing on a single segment.

Extreme Programming

Extreme programming can be defined as a typical framework for the development of agile, which was developed by Kent Black. This methodology can be adapted to various organizational structures of varying dimensions. Extreme Programming greatly emphasis values such as feedback, communication, simplicity, customer satisfaction, respect, courage and so on. This process provides trust to the developers by helping them to innovate and thereby accept the changes in the requirements of the customer, even if the developers enter the development cycle at a later date.

In Extreme Programming, it is very essential to have teamwork between your team members in the best way possible. If any problem arises, it should be solved by the team of project members, managers and executives. All the team members are necessary pieces of the puzzle, which will help in creating an environment that is fertile enough to offer high productivity and also efficiency as well. Feedback should also be collected to improve the overall development.

Extreme programming can also be defined as a disciplined approach for developing high-quality software, largely focusing on continuous delivery and speed. It helps in improving the responsiveness and quality of software in order to meet the demands of the customer. Software is delivered at frequent intervals, generally within one to three weeks. The following are some of the supporting practices of this methodology:

- Small releases
- Planning
- Customer acceptance tests
- Pair programming
- Re-factoring
- Continuous integration
- Coding standards
- Sustainable pace
- Development being test-driven

In Extreme Programming, the customer has to work closely with the development team to prioritize and define user demands. To maximize the overall productiveness, a lightweight and supportive framework is used to guide the team to deliver enterprise software that is high-quality.

Merits

Since the code that is used is very simple, it will work as an advantage in allowing for any improvement during the course of the process.

- Since the whole cycle and process is visible, it becomes easier for developers to show results in the right manner.
- In this method, the development of software turns out to be more agile than other processes.
- This methodology will help in withholding and uplifting the talent of the team members.

Demerits

- Since more focus is given on coding, less is given towards the overall design of the end product.
- If all the team members are not working in the same geographical area, then this process will not be successful.
- There is no such registry containing the list of possible errors that are maintained.

Lean Development

This kind of methodology comes directly from lean manufacturing, which was developed by the car manufacturer named Toyota. In this method, a conceptual framework is followed, which is accompanied by principles, values and also development practices that are good as well - which can all be applied to the development approach of agile. The procedure is highly flexible along with non-rigid guidelines, methods or rules. The following are some of the main principles of lean development:

- Improving the learning basis
- Eliminating unused and useless ideas and concepts
- Make decisions as fast as possible
- Make decisions as late as possible
- Help the team to be empowered
- Integrity is built into the team
- Looking over the whole process

With the help of lean development, the project team eliminates useless concepts and ideas by selecting only the features that are viable for the system. Such features are then prioritized and then are being worked upon to deliver them in incremental batches. The method stands on reliable and rapid feedback between the customers and the programmers. This emphasizes the efficiency and speed of the project.

The methodology also gives the decision making authority to smaller teams and individuals, since the process has proven to be more successful than providing the decision-making authority to the upper management. These small teams and individuals will know about the customer wants because they have been in close ties with the customer from the start of the development process.

The process also uses the team resources efficiently as well, making sure everyone is productive as possible in the team, most of the time. The method also strongly urges that the automated unit tests should be written during the same time as and when the code is written as well.

Merits

- The process helps the team to avoid any superfluous activity, thereby saving money and time in the process.
- Since the process of product development is already on the right path from the start and the team makes

most of the decisions, it improves the motivation of the team and functionalities are delivered quickly as well.

- The methodology can easily be adapted or scaled to other dimensions if required.

Demerits

- The team needs to have members who are always dedicated and extremely talented as well.

- Since all the tasks are divided into various numbers of elements, it can become easier to lose the main focus.

- The process requires a document describing the main subject of the work, as needed by the organization. Without such a document, the result can turn out to be buggy or incorrect.

Crystal

Crystal has its own family of agile methodologies, which can be described as below:

- Crystal Clear - It defines a team up to 8 persons.
- Crystal Yellow - It defines a team that has members ranging from 10 to 20 persons.
- Crystal Orange - It defines a team having members ranging from 20 to 50 persons.

- Crystal Red - It defines a team having members ranging from 50 to 1000 persons.

This methodology focuses on the main principles such as interactions, people, skills, community, talent, communication, and the likes. This helps the process to deliver in the best possible way for the development of the product or the software.

The main part of this agile methodology is to make sure that symbiosis and interaction are done on a regular basis. In order to bring efficiency to the whole development process, interaction should happen between the people that are working on the project.

The methodology was introduced by Alistair Cockburn. When compared to traditional methods, Crystal will not spend time on fixing the techniques and tools, but will instead keep the processes and the people at its core. And like other methodologies of agile, the process also offers high involvement of the user, working software being delivered at a frequent pace, elimination of bureaucracy, promoting adaptability and so on.

Merits

- Crystal ensures that problems are identified at each stage so that deliveries could be made much more frequent.

- The space to improve the characteristics of the product is always present. Therefore, time is always taken out from the development of software to discuss the ways to perfect the processes.

- Closer communication is promoted and knowledge sharing is also encouraged between team members.

- The process requires an environment that is technical enough, supported by configuration management, automated tests and also frequent integration too.

Demerits

- Since the methodology has variants of its own, the principles will also vary according to the overall size of the team.

- If teams are scattered in different areas and there is a constant need to communicate, then this process will not succeed.

- The development and planning of the process are not dependent on the requirements of the organization.

Dynamic Systems Development Method (DSDM)

DSDM can also be described as an approach known as Rapid Application Development or RAD. The main essential aspect of DSDM is to ensure that the team members are involved in the project activities and the teams are given the authority to make decisions on their own. DSDM's main focus is the frequent delivery of products.

Since the year 1994, the procedure has evolved over the years to provide a very comprehensive foundation for managing, planning, scaling and executing software development projects that are iterative in nature as well as follow agile methodologies too. DSDM is based on eight principles, which help in directing the team to create a mindset through which they will be able to deliver the project on time and within the required budget as well. It focuses on providing 80 percent of the features in almost 20 percent of the required time. The following are the principles of DSDM:

- Timely delivery
- The main business need should be focused on

- Collaboration

- Control should be demonstrated

- Quality should never be compromised

- Development should be done by means of iterations

- Firm foundations should be built first and then the rest should continue

- Clear and continuous communication

The techniques used in DSDM are:

- Prototyping

- Moscow Rules

- Time Boxing

Furthermore, DSMD has the following seven phases of working procedure:

- Pre-project

- Study of feasibility

- Study of the business end

- Interaction of a functional model

- Interaction of the build and design

- Overall implementation

- Post-project

Merits

- In DSDM, all the critical work must be done within a predefined time.

- The system requirements are always delivered and planned with the help of short time boxes. These time boxes are commonly known as iterations or sprints.

- Through this methodology, the product is delivered at a rapid pace.

Demerits

- Due to the strong emphasis on the value of time and the need for projects to be delivered on time, the team members can sometimes overlook certain parts of the development process.

Tools of Agile Project Management Application

The following list includes several tools for the Agile Management Project and also discusses the features of each of these tools.

1. Wrike

If you need to integrate the management of your project with your emails, then this is the best tool to use. Managing many different projects and dealing with multiple teams at the same time is not an easy task. This is where Wrike comes in. This tool allows you to be more flexible when handling an immense workload as it is able to scale the results and drive them quite easily, without you having to constantly supervise.

Wrike not only moves the whole process of Agile Project Management forward, but it also gives updated, and precise data and you can alter this file to enter new information whenever necessary.

With up to date and accurate reports, Wrike makes it easy for you to plan and assess a project and also provides some extra features like daily customization and supportive tools for collaboration, which are designed to help you and your team manage work in a more efficient

2. Proggio

While the Agile Project Management is an all-inclusive approach, Proggio is a tool that builds on this and focuses on the interactions of the people associated with the project, instead of the tasks involved. When you use Proggio, your team will have a common purpose and that will drive them to manage the workload and reach the goal.

This is what the tool aims at and such a system is only possible because of some amazing features like, project visualization, collaboration, automatic, patented analysis, and insights to help improve the project.

3. Asana

A complete Agile Project Management tool, Asana provides a platform for all teams to organize, plan, collaborate and keep a track of the projects they are working on. It is one of the simplest tools in terms of applications and is very easy to use.

It is free for a maximum of thirty members in a team and you will not even need an email account to start using this tool. Asana allows its users to create their own space for work and you can attach notes, write comments and give tags to each of the projects as you see fit.

4. Nuvro

Managing a project can seem to be a tiring job, but the tools of Agile Project Management simply that a lot. Nuvro is one such tool that helps you be more efficient when it comes to project management. It creates tasks and subtasks and automatically assigns them to team members who will be able to tackle them. Transparency and accountability are the two things that you can be sure of while using this tool.

5. JIRA

While working on a project, keeping your work bug free and protecting it from potential attacks is extremely important. JIRA is an Agile Project Management tool that does exactly that. JIRA searches for bugs and any problems that might threaten your data and compromise your progress. It can also be used to manage your project and deal with different mobile and software developments.

All of its functions and features are listed on a dashboard and these are designed to tackle many different issues at the same time. Using JIRA, you will be able to understand what kind of issues you are dealing with as well as the attributes of those issues and you will also get a clear picture of the workflow along with that of the various screens and fields related to your project.

6. Agilean

This Agile Project Management tool is a project software solution that is really great for IT companies that are not too large in nature. Along with being a software solution, Agilean is also a SaaS enterprise workflow automation with features that can make work much easier for any enterprise.

Using these features, you will be able to plan a project becomes much easier, followed by executing that plan properly and then monitoring the work. Agilean allows you to not only come up retrospective analysis of a project but also impediments, release management and with this tool, you will get visualized reports of the work in progress along with stand up meeting automation.

7. Drag

A key part of the Agile Project Management is to stay organized and Drag provides a way of doing that by converting your Gmail into several Task Lists. These Task Lists are extremely convenient and they help you to have a clear idea of how the project is progressing and what are the things that you still need to do.

Drag is actually an extension of Chrome and it easily transforms your Gmail inbox into an accessible workspace that you can manage without any trouble. Drag Team, which will be launched on December 18, will allow all teams working on a project to collaborate using just their Gmail accounts.

8. Binfire

A project management software that supports not only Agile Project Management, but also other methodologies like Hybrid and Waterfall Project Management, Binfire is a pretty versatile tool. It allows you to collaborate and provides real time reports of all those collaborations along with several other features like Burndown charts, project folders, a message board, and an interactive whiteboard to discuss all project related matters with your team members, as well as collaborative PDF mark-ups along with target notifications, and status updates.

Other than these features, as a part of the whole project management procedure, Binfire also helps track bugs so that your information remains protected and you are aware of any issues that might jeopardize your work progress.

9. VivifyScrum

Great for both small and large enterprises, VivifyScrum is an Agile Project Management tool that offers customizable Scrum boards which are very useful for collaborations. These boards will allow you to work using different Scrum practices, Sprints, and even Product backlog management.

There are also Kanban boards available for those who find them more convenient. You can also use item cards to provide information on each of the tasks associated with the ongoing project and even share necessary files. This tool will allow you to manage different projects at the same time and with the help of the advanced team management feature you will easily be able to assign the tasks to people most suitable for them. Vivify has an internal time tracker which creates logs, monitoring the progress of every team member and it also provides you with invoices that can be sent straight to your clients.

10. Backlog

This Agile Project Management tool is a complete solution to managing your work. It provides features that will help you deal with supervising different tasks, tracking bugs and other issues and also version control. These features include Gantt charts, sub tasking, and custom issue fields along with Burndown charts, Wikis, and Git & SVN repositories that allow you to not only track and manage, but also review, release and even document the code.

The tool also gives notifications that help every developer to stay on top of the work. Introducing efficiency and convenience to workflows and code management, Backlog successfully brings the entire organization together to make sure that every collaboration reaches its full potential.

11. Trello

One of the most popular and frequently used Agile Project Management tools, Trello's application, which is supported even on mobiles, is based upon the Kanban methodology where each project is shown as a board and all information related to the particular project is listed on that board. You can pay for a premium account to use Trello, but even if you have a free account, you will have access to most of its features.

The lists of information have progressive cards that you can easily drag-and-drop whenever you need to and you can also give these cards to all team members working on that project so that they are aware of the progress or any recent developments. This tool also has a few smaller functions like colored labels, writing comments, and notes, reminders for due dates, and preparing checklists, and integrating with some other applications, which simplifies the work process.

12. OneDesk

Agile Project Management is based on a holistic approach and this is a tool that reflects that. OneDesk not only allows you to manage your projects easily but it also helps to stay in touch with your clients so that you are able to provide any service they might require with the project is at its developmental stages. The application of OneDesk is easy with Gantt charts, notifications about work progress and updates, timesheets which help in tracking, accurate reports, task timers, exporting of tasks, roadmaps, and plan releases.

13. Kanbanize

Transparency is of the utmost importance in any project. This Kanban software brings about transparency not only in the whole enterprise but also in each team working on one aspect of the project. Kanbanize is a great tool for all companies looking to organize their workflow and keep a check on the updates, and developments that are happening across their projects.

The whole system of Agile Project Management is primarily about efficiency, and Kanbanize, with its customizable project boards and information lists, takes that one step further. It provides timelines that you can use to organize your tasks and create workflows that are more manageable within a particular time period and there is also an analytics module available that allows you to have insights into how you can improve the project by taking note of a few metrics like cycle time, team output, and lead time.

14. nTask:

This Agile Project Management tool allows you to make checklists, collaborate with different teams working on different tasks, schedule meetings with members and well with clients, and share all relevant files. When working on a project, you should be spending your time developing ideas and working towards the end goal, instead of wasting too much time managing tasks and taking care of logistics. nTask simplifies this part of your work and helps you tackle the tasks in a quick and efficient way so that you can stop worrying about project management and actually focus on the more important aspects.

15. Pivotal Tracker

If you are involved in a software developing project, then this Agile Project Management tool is for you. Pivotal Tracker provides visuals of each of your projects and the progress is depicted as stories on virtual cards.

This will help you to understand where your project stands and organize all the tasks in ways that can be easily managed over a certain time period. The tool also provides a platform for you to discuss the project with concerned clients. You can assess your team's work and pace and then divide each of those stories created on the visual cards accordingly for the future.

16. Assembla

This tool is for software developers who are working on cloud-based tasks and code management. You will want to use Assembla if you wish to drive your project from the usual Scrum Agile towards an organized, well distributed system that is continuous and can be scaled as and when required.

This tool provides Subversion hosting for Git, P4 along with Dropbox integration and Agile task management. Starting from planning a project and putting that plan to action to actually reaping benefits and obtaining proper results, Assembla can be used for all tasks related to project management, especially with its additional features which allow you to easily upload media files which are quite large, manage various code reviews, and keep track of your work by documenting its progress. Assembla also allows you to integrate your tasks with other applications like GitHub or Slack.

17. StoriesOnBoard

Visualizing project plans makes work much easier. StoriesOnBoard is an Agile Project Management tool that helps you create visuals of your tasks using their "user story mapping" feature. This feature is ideal for product owners and it is integrated with various other tools like JIRA, Trello, Azure DevOps, Pivotal Tracker and GitHub.

Practical Implications of Agile Project Management

Planning a project can be tough, especially as it involves several detailed tasks that need to complete to reach the final goal of the process. Agile Project management offers a process of project planning that is not only simplified but also efficient as it will help you to get your work organized in no time at all.

The approach that Agile Project management has towards the process of planning a project and organizing the workflow, is iterative or frequentative in nature, which makes things really easy and convenient for all team members involved.

What is the Agile Project Management Method or Approach?

When you are using Agile Project Management, you get to plan your project process by creating various steps, instead of having to complete a single task all at once. The members of the teams working on various different tasks can collaborate with one another and even with stakeholders easily.

The Agile Project Management approach also enables every team member to keep a track of their work input and you will be able to monitor the recent developments and the progress of the project. Agile Project Management involves several methodologies which bring order to your enterprise so that you are able to deal with all kinds of changes and use every opportunity to create a proper work environment. The most commonly used methodologies are:

- Scrum
- Kanban
- Extreme Programming (XP)
- Adaptive Project Framework (APF)

The flexibility of the Agile Project Management Method or Approach

The older approach towards project management was designed to handle simple projects which did not involve too many tasks or subtasks. This approach, also known as the "waterfall" method needed a working prototype before it could determine the other requirements for the project plan to work.

This is actually not possible as most of the time, the project does not go according to its original plan. The project management plan involved, therefore, needs to be flexible as it will need to accommodate adjustments and various changes as the tasks are completed and the project proceeds. This is exactly what the Agile Project Management method of approach does;

- It allows you to make necessary changes whenever and wherever you see fit, while also guiding you through difficult tasks.

- It helps you organize your project, which while being efficient, is not set in concrete and you can easily fit it at your convenience.

- With regular reports and accurate analysis, the Agile Project Management approach always provides you with an opportunity to identify the shortcomings in your project plan and implement a more consistent and useful plan of action.

- The Agile Project Management method also provides a perfect opportunity for teams to collaborate on different tasks. But unlike the "waterfall" method where the entire team was focused on one particular task (making the process far more lengthy), on using the Agile Project Management approach, you will have specific tasks assigned to people who are most suitable for them, so that the entire project can be completed faster, not to mention, more efficiently.

Structure Of The Agile Project Management Plan

The structure of the Agile Management plan is divided into three different categories. If you are using it, then you will need to be aware of the guiding principles of this method, the recommended division of team members and the process of project management.

1. Guiding Principles

   - The continuous and proper delivery of finished product to ensure customer satisfaction.
   - Accommodating changes even when the project is in its final stages.
   - Frequent delivery of projects.
   - Coordination and collaboration between team members.
   - Providing a secure environment for team members to come up with innovative approaches and apply them to relevant projects.
   - Free flow of information between teams and effective face-to-face conversations.

- Keeping a track of all developments and the progress of the project.

2. Team Members

- Skilled in one or more areas with enough experience and a wide range of knowledge when it comes to their subject.

- Adaptable in even dire situations and are able to provide great output.

- Have basic knowledge and skills outside their area of expertise so that they can lend a hand to other teams when necessary.

- Will prioritize the success of the team over individual achievements.

3. Process of Project Management

- Planning ahead, keeping in mind the purpose of the project and allowing enough room for changes to be made in the future.

- Creating a roadmap which will create smaller steps, each containing specific tasks to enhance efficiency.

- Release planning before starting the actual project and have the feature release re-evaluated at certain intervals.

- Maintain visual documentation and provide reports of how everyone has fared in each task so that there are transparency and scope for improvement within a team

Staff Issue after Adopting Agile

When you first introduce the Agile Project Management method, your staff might be a little hesitant. This is actually one of the problems that many organizations face with Agile. You might hire professionals who are trained in Agile and they will not be able to fit in with your team members. This might lead to some kind of inefficiency when it comes to the completion of the project. Now, if this happens, then possibly for your organization, it will be better to train your existing staff in Agile and get them to obtain Agile Project Management certificates so that they are able to take care of the management process on their own. But then, even here some complications might arise.

Your staff might not be ready to adopt this new plan of action which is bound to introduce some radical changes to the existing management patterns. However, with either of these cases, you will need experienced people if you want the Agile Project Management plan to work. Those who are not experienced in the method will not be able to cope with the different approach and that will affect the entire project.

So if you do have staff issues, which many organizations have in the beginning, try figuring out which way you should introduce the methodologies so that everybody is able to understand and get on board with the ideas and the changes (or if your staff is willing, then you can simply hire professionals to help you organize your projects).

Market Implications of Agile Project Management

In the marketing industry, the Agile Project Management plan analyses existing situations in a given context and uses the data to come up with several hopeful prospects. When you are trying to evaluate the market, Agile helps in providing solutions and upgrades that will take care of most issues, allowing you to go forward with your project.

A marketing organization using Agile, can organize multiple campaigns and run them simultaneously without compromising any aspect and also evaluate the outputs so that the information can be used to improve future tasks. The Agile Project Management method provides a steady speed to the workflow which is essential in the marketing context. In keeping with this, there is a constant flow of opportunities and the constant use of tests helps teams to stay on top of their work.

Cost of Agile Certificates

To use the Agile Project Management method, you will have to be trained in specific agile skills and for this, you can obtain certain certifications. The list below discusses a few common agile certifications and the costs involved.

- PMI-ACP (Agile Certified Practitioner from the Project Management Institute) is for professionals in project management who work in organizations looking to adopt the Agile method. The paper based testing format costs $385 while the computer based testing costs $495.

- StrategyEx Certificate in Agile is an Associate or Master certificate offered in partnership with George Washington University. It involves many courses like Agile Practices for Product Owners, Delivering Agile Projects with Scrum, Estimation and Planning, Product Management, each costing $1645.

- Certificate from International Consortium for Agile which will help you become an expert on Scrum, Extreme Programming, and Kanban. Each certificate costs $60.

When Should You Adopt Agile Project Management?

While the Agile Project Management approach does make work easier, adopting this approach will lead to several implications. The organization which is going to adopt the method will need to prepare for various changes at the management level, especially involving the distribution of information. All methodologies of the Agile Project Management approach work primarily on the principle of transparency and whichever one you choose to implement will involve the free flow of information relevant to the completion of a particular task.

This approach towards the process of project planning and management also involves collaboration on specific tasks. The collaboration can be between teams or even between your organization and your clients. Collaborating on tasks gives rise to new ideas and it also provides clarity on how the project is progressing.

Therefore, if your organization has maintained proper management practices then adopting the agile method will not be a problem. You will have to make sure that all teams are skilled in Agile and that they understand how it works.

How to Measure Agile Project Management Success?

There are currently numerous companies out there trying to leverage various metrics to measure the overall success of their organization. But, when it comes to leveraging the metrics of agile project management, things are a lot more complex than you would actually think it to be.

When you start an agile project, you already have to make plans on ways to measure success because without measuring success in the right manner, your project can't proceed forward. Furthermore, when it comes to agile, there's not a single method or metric that will be perfect for organizations of all sizes and kinds. Keeping those factors in mind, the following are some of the most important metrics by which you can measure the success of your business' agile project management implementation.

Timely Delivery

Timely delivery is one of the most important metrics that most organizations use to measure the success of agile project management. But since agile already relies on time management to finish projects within schedules - in this case, timely delivery is meant by the work that is done in accordance with the overall expectations of what is about to be delivered.

This helps in improving the visibility aspect of agile project management in regards to the work that is being done and delivered on a consistent basis over time. This helps team members to be more encouraged about their work and therefore deal with complex situations beforehand.

The Defects

When you take any project into consideration, you have to take care of its defects as well. Defects can be part of any project. But, with the help of agile project management, your team will be able to reduce or minimize the number of defects that largely occur. You can easily track the defect metrics and allow the development team to learn and know the way it can avoid such defects and also rectify the same as well.

The number of defects and the increase or decrease in such defects will help you know the overall progress of the project. It will help you to spark discussions with your development team, thereby improving the overall techniques during the sprint retrospectives.

The satisfaction of the Customer

This metric is used to measure how much the customer is satisfied with the overall progress of agile project management. Using this metric to measure agile projects is the real idea that lies behind the whole agile philosophy. Agile relies on customer feedback to develop better and more efficient products by mainly focusing on the needs and requirements of the customers.

The agile methodology generally works to deliver the best value to the end-user through its working product or software. You can measure customer satisfaction in various different ways, which includes usage statistics, an increase in the number of sales, user opinions, and reviews and the likes.

The Quality of the Product

It can be a little more difficult to measure the quality of the product developed through agile procedures, with the help of such metrics. Like it was mentioned before, the methodology of agile relies upon the creation of value for the end-user. Therefore, it means that even though there is a greater emphasis on the quality of the product, the most challenging part is the way you can measure the obtained success.

You can do this by starting to look at the overall customer satisfaction along with the growth rates in terms of revenues and also the other technical aspects of the agile environment's testing phases. When it comes to agile practices and policies, the development team focuses on building software with the help of quality product integration right from the start.

When the development team allows for continuous testing methods throughout the lifecycle of the product, it ensures that the software or the product is being developed in the right manner, which will ensure the right kind of quality at the end of the product of software lifecycle.

The Value Created For the Business

It's essential to measure the business value which is being created through the help of the various agile policies and practices. It has been mentioned and recognized in the Agile Manifesto regarding the significance of business values in many agile principles. When you're planning to measure business value, the ambition should be very clear about what you need. This is because creating value for the business is all about knowing whether the requirements for compliance or contract has been fulfilled.

Therefore, if you can apply the metric of business value to measure the kind of features that are to be delivered by the development team, then it will help in measuring the whole project's success in an effective manner.

The Overall Product's Scope

The success of your agile project can also be measured with the help of the project's scope too. The scope of the project will contain all the necessary requirements and features, as an integral part of the agile project management. When you will be setting a goal regarding the developments that are to be made in the upcoming three months, then it can get quite rewarding when tracking the status of the project and also completing the relevant tasks related to it as well.

When you'll be receiving updates in real-time regarding the benefits of your project being completed, it will benefit everyone involved in the development of products or software. You will be easily visualizing the success of the project and also its overall progression towards the finishing line.

The Product's Visibility

Without a shadow of a doubt, visibility can be a massive factor and also an essential metric in various agile policies and practices. Good product visibility will also lead to better success in the overall project as well. The product's visibility is based on the overall transparency of product development and transparency is very significant in building long-term trust as well. In simpler terms, the plans of the project should be available to all and everyone should have access to the progress of the project, so that trust between team members could increase multi-folds. Following that method, everyone involved in the project's success, including the managers and stakeholders can provide their perspective on the project's success.

You have to make sure that the features of the project should be portrayed side by side with the current project plan in mind so that everyone could see the overall success. Moreover, with the help of visibility, the alignment of different teams becomes easy. When more than one team is working on the development of a particular project, then with the help of visibility, you can spark mutual understanding and cooperation between the team members and the teams as well. This will in-turn give a boost to the overall success of the project

The Return on Investment Or R.O.I

Return on investment can be defined as the income that is generated by the product or the software that is being developed. If the product costs less money to produce, which means that the company had to spend less money overall, then it can be said that the product's ROI is high.

In terms of agile projects, the concept of ROI is different than what is being used in traditional projects. With the help of agile projects, you can easily allow the product or software in hand to help you generate income from the first iteration or release itself. The revenue will continue to increase with every release version. ROI is indeed a great metric for a company to appreciate its development team and also the overall value of the project that is ongoing as well.

With the help of ROI metrics, organizations can decide whether to fund or scrap a project completely. The ROI potential is what most companies look at. The ROI of individual projects, as well as projects for the company as a whole, can be tracked by the company.

The Overall Productivity

When working in an agile environment, it is very essential that productivity is kept at an all-time high. It can also be a very useful metric to monitor and look after the overall success of the project as well. In an agile environment, productivity is measured in terms of overall output.

Thus, you can easily figure out the impact of productivity by looking at the requirements that are completed or done. If a team is high on productivity, then the requirements will be done fast and quick. If productivity is less, then more time will be required to complete the same requirements.

The Overall Predictability

Predictability is another one of the most important factors when measuring the success of agile project management. You can measure predictability with the help of the velocity trend. Velocity trend can be defined as the maximum amount of work that a scrum team or an agile team can pull off or complete in each agile sprints.

When you'll measure this trend for around three to four months, you'll come to know about the amount of the work that has been done or completed at a pace that is sustainable enough for the development team. In case the metric of velocity differs on a drastic basis, then it can mean that there are a number of factors that can be responsible for such behavior, including team changes, teams getting used to the new work and so on.

Success can also be measured on the number of user stories that are being completed on a regular basis per week, which will also be a nice indicator of predictability too.

The Duration Of The Project

There's no doubt that the agile project is done much quicker than normal traditional waterfall projects. Thus, by allowing the project to start quicker and at a much faster rate will help you cut all the bloatware that is unnecessary. Bloatware, in this case, is referred to as the requirements that are not significant and are not required. In this way, the project teams following agile project management can deliver the project at a much faster rate than ever before.

You will need to measure the time duration required for the whole project to complete to know the success of the process.

The Overall Project Cost

The cost of the agile projects will depend on the actual duration of the project. The longer will be the duration, the greater the cost that will arise as well. But, since projects following agile methodologies take less time to complete than traditional policy-following projects, the cost will also be on the lesser side.

Companies or organizations can use the various cost metrics to plan their budgets, determine the overall return on investment and also know the time to exercise the redeployment of capital to boost the working productivity. If the project cost stays within the budget, then it will be called a success.

The Process Improvement

Agile principles and policies depend on a crucial philosophy, which includes continuous improvement of the project development in hand. The development team should always strive to be better at all times. But measuring the process improvement will be not possible if the outcome of the project is not measured at all. Therefore, success needs to be measured at every sprint ending to know the current status of the project.

You need to use the combination of the above-mentioned steps, including predictability, productivity, and velocity to know whether the development team is putting in the hard work.

Finally, it should be kept in mind that keeping track of the various agile metrics is always beneficial to the organization or business entity. It will help the company to choose the right team and also the project for future success. You'll need an overview that is balanced in every field in order to make decisions which will work in favor of the development team following agile practices and policies, and also the project itself.

You need to apply these metrics in the best possible manner to help in counting the overall success of the agile project management implementation.

Conclusion

It has indeed been a long journey when talking about agile project management in all its glory. It started with the history of agile project management and how the concept was necessary to build a great future for upcoming projects and developers. Building on that foundation, the principles of agile project management were discussed as a result.

Moving on, it was time to know about the definition of agile project management and the need to be agile to produce better results. The scope, as well as the benefits of the agile concept, were discussed along with it too.

Diving a little deeper, the principles of agile project management were discussed in greater detail, combined with the benefits of agile project management too. This allowed you to learn about the reasons why agile is better and much more preferred in the current development world than traditional waterfall strategies. Moreover, the advantages of agile were also pitted against traditional procedures as well.

On to the next lesson, the challenges of agile project management were discussed in greater detail, to help you learn the various obstacles which can be avoided to see the full potential of agile project management being unleashed.

Coming to the part of the implementation, it was time to know and learn about how an agile environment operates and the way you can structure the whole developmental team efficiently. The methods to create agile values and rules were also shared.

Next up, the effective implementation of agile project management was discussed in detail, roping in various concepts and ideas. The phases of agile project management were also discussed so that you can know the process makes its progress slowly and steadily. Banking on the same idea, the reasons for which the process could fail were also examined and talked about.

Moreover, the various agile methodologies along with all their respective merits and demerits were discussed. Finally, the whole journey was rounded off by discussing the various ways or methods through which you can measure the success of agile project management.

* 9 7 9 8 6 1 1 0 0 7 5 7 0 *